PRAISE FOR *FIND YOUR STRENGTH*

'A short, wonderfully readable and timely plunge into the ailments of the modern world, salved by deep insights into ancient wisdoms. Part *Bhagavad Gita*, part *Bridget Jones's Diary*, there's a delightful walk-in-the-forest cameo appearance from Batman as well.' David Leser, author of *Women, Men and the Whole Damn Thing*

'A great read ... will be warmly welcomed for the insights it offers.' Abbie Cornish, actor

'Healing, calming and empowering. Rachael and her work in this world are such a gift.' Cassie Mendoza-Jones, author of *You Are Enough*

'I am no yogi, I am deeply inflexible, but this book opened me right up. I love the idea of investigating ancient practices and connecting them with modern struggles. The more we evolve, I have noticed, the more we seek to be more like the people who were here first. Rachael plays to her strengths in *Find Your Strength*, using her piercing and observant wit, cradled by a tough humility, to bring us a handbook for the now. Namaste!' Brendan Cowell, actor, screenwriter and author

Affirm
press

Currently a presenter on Australia's beloved *Play School*, Rachael is an award-winning storyteller working across many forms, writing, acting and producing for international screen and stage for over two decades. While storytelling is her career, yoga is Rachael's passion. Having been handed her first books on yoga philosophy and Buddhism at a young age while struggling with mental health issues, they have become the foundation of her entire life. A yoga teacher for over a decade now, Rachael's greatest passion is translating this ancient, powerful wisdom in a way that speaks to everyone.

Dearest George

May you

Find Your Strength

+ your spark ✦

RACHAEL COOPES

♡ *Rachael Coopes*

Affirm
press

Affirmpress

books that leave an impression

Published by Affirm Press in 2022
28 Thistlethwaite Street, South Melbourne,
Boon Wurrung Country, VIC 3205
affirmpress.com.au
10 9 8 7 6 5 4 3 2 1

A catalogue record for this
book is available from the
National Library of Australia

NATIONAL
LIBRARY
OF AUSTRALIA

Title: Find Your Strength / Rachael Coopes, author
ISBN: 9781922626523 (hardback)

Cover design by Emily Thiang
Author photo by LEEROY.T
Typeset by Post Pre-press Group, Brisbane
Printed and bound in China by RR Donnelley Asia Printing Solutions Ltd.

To my warrior mum, who helped me find my strength.
My great love, Gabriel, who showed me my spark.
And Blue Connelly, who will always be my guide.

Contents

Introduction

'Only to the extent that we expose ourselves
over and over to annihilation can that which
is indestructible be found in us.'
Pema Chodron

No matter who you are or where you're from, there comes a moment in life when you find yourself on the battlefield, having to channel your inner strength and fight when you simply can't. When all you want to do is lay down your weapons and not 'adult' anymore. This book will serve as a guide to finding your inner warrior so you can pick yourself up, adult to the best of your ability and face whatever challenges life throws at you with grace.

We will use tried-and-tested ancient teachings to understand many different ways to access this strength. There will be reflection questions and practical exercises for you to apply this knowledge in a tangible way. You will hear personal stories (and discover my love for Disney) in order to connect to some of the concepts that may otherwise feel esoteric. You will also walk away with a toolkit you can access at any time.

This book is not just a survival manual. Rather, a resource empowering you to embrace life's shitshow moments. We will explore different ways to understand, and access, inner strength. Some concepts may resonate with you more than others, because each one of us has different work to do.

I don't want you to be under any illusions that it's going to be easy or that there are any quick fixes to connect to your true power. I don't believe there is such a thing. Quick fixes are generally that – they bandaid our scratches, ignoring the gaping wounds elsewhere that just won't heal. It's going to require contemplation, courage and commitment. But I believe it's the most important thing you can do in this lifetime – to discover who and what you really are and where your limitless strength lies – so you can spend the precious time you have living your life from a place of fearlessness. Knowing that whatever shitstorm you find yourself in, you have an anchor to weather it all. Because, the reality is, you'll either become a *warrior* or a *worrier*.

The wisdom I'm going to share with you has been practised and applied over thousands of years. None of it comes from me. It's all drawn from the ancient teachings of yoga that I've spent decades sitting with, as well as studying with incredible teachers who made it digestible (especially Manorama D'Alvia). I personally know it works, because it's given me strength to weather my own stormy seas across decades – most potently, surviving single parenthood.

A few years ago, I found myself very pregnant and very alone, facing a future as a single mother that I hadn't planned. My partner and I had separated, but not in a Gwyneth Paltrow 'conscious uncoupling' kinda way. It was more like a *Game-of-Thrones*-final-episode vibe. My pubic bone decided to copycat, and separate, too (which is some high-level *Game-of-Thrones* pain, let me tell you). My son Gabriel was born, screaming his little lungs out, which he continued to do ... all the time.

He never slept, wouldn't eat and cried a lot. I wondered if I'd ever sleep, or smile, again.

And then things got worse. I did smile – I had to. With bills to pay, in the middle of a bleak, freezing Canberra winter, I was back on tour with *Play School Live* concerts. I crawled on stage, smile plastered, in brightly coloured clothes hiding a body covered in psoriasis, singing 'If You're Happy and You Know It' to a sea of ecstatic toddlers. While I was on stage, my grandpa was backstage rocking Gabriel in his pram, also singing and pulling funny faces. I was so very grateful to have him there, my beloved Grandpa. He was my greatest champion and ally.

Back in my hotel room, lying on a floor covered in towels with a projectile-vomiting, non-sleeping, reflux baby in tow, I fell apart. I felt exhausted and alone, on the battlefield of solo working parenthood, with no idea how the actual f%^& I was going to do this. My very Catholic grandpa had given me a card when I was young, and I'd kept it all my life. It had a picture of a little boat on a choppy ocean, dangerously close to a jagged, rocky sea cliff. It read: 'God will protect you, but you have to row away from the rocks.'

One of the primary yogic texts, the *Bhagavad Gita*, is set on a battlefield. Not in a pre-COVID-imagined utopia. Not on a yoga retreat in Bali drinking smoothies. On a battlefield. In the text, our warrior hero, Arjuna, surveys the battlefield he is about to fight on and has a panic attack. He says to his guide, Krishna (who happens to be God): 'I can't do this. I can't fight.'

Now, you'd think that the universe/God, in all its peace-loving wisdom, would say something like: 'You're right. Let's just love each other, kiss and make up, and go home.' But no. Krishna tells Arjuna that he has to fight. *But*, he says, he will teach him yoga in the process. He will give him tools to navigate the battlefield clearly, courageously and consciously.

There are many times in life when throwing down your weapons in surrender is not an option and you have to fight. Things may have fallen apart. You may have lost everything. You may have to choose between a few shitty options. Or maybe there's no choice and you have to do something you really don't want to do. No one else can do it for you. Even with loving family and friends, even with the wind in your sails, even with an army behind you like Arjuna had in the *Bhagavad Gita*. There are times in life when you have to warrior up and go it alone. You have to row away from the rocks. These were my first lessons on the battlefield of single parenthood.

So, I got up off the floor, kissed my momentarily sleeping baby (very gently so I wouldn't wake him), had a shower, texted Alex Papps – my beloved, supportive co-presenter on tour – and asked him if he could get me some chocolate and chips from the vending machine in the car park. I didn't know how on earth I was going to survive this chapter. But I knew chocolate, and the *Gita*, was a really good start.

CHAPTER 1

You Have to Fight

'One who shirks action does not attain freedom; no
one can gain perfection by abstaining from work.
Indeed, there is no one who rests for even an instant;
all creatures are driven to action by their own nature.'
Bhagavad Gita 3:4 and 3:5 (translated by Eknath Easwaran)

The *Bhagavad Gita* is an epic poem that is part of a vast literary masterpiece called the *Mahabharata*. Authorship is disputed, but it is generally agreed that it was compiled by a great sage called Vyasa between the 2nd and 4th centuries BCE. It is considered one of the primary texts of Hinduism and yoga, a significant contribution to literature and one of the most remarkable, and widely read, books on philosophy. The *Gita*, as it is warmly referred to, has been a trusted guide for many prominent artists, thinkers, philosophers, politicians, scientists and leaders across the ages. From Mahatma Gandhi and Ralph Waldo Emerson to Carl Jung, Albert Einstein and Robert Oppenheimer, it has provided valuable wisdom for great minds.

I discovered the *Gita* a few decades ago as a yogi. Over many years studying with my teachers, contemplating different translations, I have fallen in love with this book. The strength it has given me is insurmountable.

But I always struggled with its first big teaching: you have to fight. It seemed contrary to what the spiritual path should be all about. I didn't sign up for more fighting! I was tired of fighting. I'd come to yoga and meditation to escape fighting. Didn't the great sages understand that? That we were all doing our best to not fight anymore. That we were running, sunning, walking, talking, boxing, detoxing, surfing, rebirthing, meditating, ice bathing, CrossFitting, knitting, oxygen chamber-ing and infrared sauna-ing to get more peace in our lives? Of course, they understood completely. This is why it's the first lesson on Arjuna's spiritual path.

You Have to Act

Here's the inconvenient truth of being human: you have to take action. In every moment of every day, you have to do something. Even if that something is choosing to do nothing, it's still an action.

Each day when you wake up, it all begins. You open your eyes, the senses ignite and lights, camera, action – it's showtime. The phone, the dog, the kids, the coffee, the organising ... within minutes, the camera is rolling and the show has begun.

But are you running the show or are you watching your life unfold from the couch? And if you aren't the showrunner of your own life, then who the hell is? I don't know about you, but I want to be in the director's chair. I want to be running the show; I don't want the show running me.

In some of the greatest film performances of all time, the actors are seemingly doing nothing. But that nothing speaks volumes. It's an art as a performer to do nothing and make it mean everything. Inaction is still a choice, and a powerful one at that. When I say 'inaction', I'm not talking about the necessity of sometimes being still. There is definitely a time to pull in, to sit with things and contemplate what the next right thing to do is (we'll talk more about that later). But inaction in our lives, most of the time, is just unconscious action – we're choosing not to act for some reason or to delay something we know we have to do (hello, procrastination).

So, if you have to take action, may it be conscious. May it be skilful. May you be an active viewer. May you not phone your life in, doing thousands of tiny actions without even realising it. Otherwise, it's just activity. And unconscious activity, my friends, is the best way to hand your precious life over and wonder why you are exhausted all the time. This may be why you are tired and disempowered, searching outside yourself for more strength. Why coffee is your best friend. Why you hand over your pay cheques willingly to acupuncturists, naturopaths, chiropractors, masseuses, kinesiologists and all manner of other 'ologists', desperate for them to fill you back up.

And why the journey of tapping into your inner strength starts here, with you waking up.

Waking Up

The first step on the path to becoming a warrior is to wake up to the present moment. Don't fairytale it, waiting for Prince Charming to rouse you with a kiss (although I would argue that this is a great idea, and relationships are a brutally productive way to wake you up – more on that to come). Don't set an alarm and hit snooze. Start now, today, in this very moment. Wake up and choose which actions to consciously take. Then do those actions on purpose in every moment of every day.

Mindfulness master Jon Kabat-Zinn defines mindfulness as exactly this: paying attention, on purpose, in the present moment with no judgement. Now, that is way easier said than done because it involves us sitting in whatever arises. Being in the present moment – good or bad – and observing what is happening around you.

To wake up, you have to notice you're asleep. Observe how much of your life you are sleepwalking away, while throwing your energy around like it's confetti – like you're on some episode of *Oprah* or *Ellen*: 'You get some of my energy! YOU get some of my energy!' – until you have none left. Sad face.

Burnout

Welcome to the modern age of burnout. A 2021 Forbes study found that more than 50 per cent of the US population experienced burnout. A worldwide survey commissioned by California-based work-management app Asana showed that Australia had one of the highest rates of burnout of any country in 2020, at 77 per cent of the population. Surrounded by stimuli at levels we've never encountered before, while grappling with a rapidly changing pandemic landscape and working ourselves into the ground, it's no surprise.

There are so many things we need to address in order to combat the endemic burnout in society today. I know we can only control so much. The world is set up in a way that is not conducive to preserving our precious energy resources. But that's why it's so important to manage our own supplies as best we can.

This miraculous vehicle you're getting around in is only going to travel as far, and drive as well, as the service and maintenance it's receiving. It's a complex conduit with many layers, all requiring your care and attention. Like a car, you have to look after everything, from the engine to the tyres, oil, water, interior and exterior. Our instrument is the same, but different. Let's start with the body of the vehicle.

Let's Get Physical

When it comes to managing our vitality, it all starts with the outermost sheath. This is where nutrition, hydration, rest and exercise directly determine the amount of energy and strength you have. The more healthy, fit, well slept, nourished and hydrated the physical body is, the clearer your thinking and the more vitality you'll have. It's as simple as that. Prioritising care of this chunk of flesh you get around in every day is crucial if you're interested in harnessing your vital strength.

What are you putting in, and on, your body? Especially during busy times or peak periods of stress, as that's when you generally drop the ball, make less-nourishing food choices, drink too much (alcohol), worry more, sleep less and avoid exercise. I know it feels counterintuitive in those shitty times to look after yourself – the mind is searching for escape and temporary pleasure, among other things – but you need to load up on the good stuff to support you through the bad stuff. I'm not going to give you advice on what the 'good stuff' and 'bad stuff' is, because I'm not a qualified medical practitioner, nutritionist or naturopath. And, you know, what the world needs now is yet another person, like me, giving you a smoothie recipe. All I'll say is this: I think we all know when we are nourishing the body and when we are not. Get real with yourself. If you want to be stronger, there's no way around addressing the state of your physical health.

Exercise has been proven to directly foster not only physical strength but also mental fortitude on a physiological level. Associate professor of psychiatry at Harvard Medical School, John Ratey, undertook extensive research that revealed exercise triggers biological changes that encourage brain cells to bind to one another. This directly determines the brain's ability to adapt to challenges. Aerobic activity, in particular, affects adaptation; therefore it's an indispensable tool for anyone who wants to reach their full potential.

If we're talking about reaching your full potential through aerobic activity, my recommendation would be to put on a shiny white leotard, sweatband and some matching white boots. Play a certain 1981 film clip and, just like Olivia Newton-John, let's get physical. (If you haven't yet heard and seen the musical art that is this piece of pop culture, you're welcome.)

Every Breath You Take

Research shows that becoming conscious of how you breathe can change your physiology. One particular study illustrated that by simply slowing the breath down, there were improvements to emotional control and psychological wellbeing in subjects. These included *increased* relaxation, pleasantness, vigour and alertness, as well as *reduced* symptoms of anxiety, depression, anger and confusion. Another study determined

YOU HAVE TO FIGHT

that conscious breath helps the brain grow new connections, enhances our attention and improves brain health. Even a few mindful breaths a day can make radical differences to your life by waking you up, bringing you into the present and improving your overall vitality.

Mind Your Own Mind

Of all the layers that form our vehicle, the mind layer is infinitely more powerful than the others. It uses energy with every thought, feeling and emotion. So, if you want more inner strength, start inside your mind. The first thing you need to notice is where you are placing your attention.

Where attention goes, energy flows. The modern world pulls your interest in a thousand different directions all the time and, as it does, your energy follows. It is literally stealing your life force, or 'prana' in Sanskrit, and you are allowing it to do so. Most of the time, we are not even conscious of *where* that energy goes. It gets hijacked by a thousand things, people, events, all vying for your precious attention.

Yes, I know, most of us have to work. Yes, we live in 'unprecedented' times. Yes, we are subject to constant distraction, with multi-billion-dollar companies designed to steal our attention, and profiting from doing so. The odds are stacked against us. But if you are exhausted all the time, largely because you are not controlling where your awareness goes, that is on you. The next chapter looks at how to reclaim your prana once and for all.

It's time to be the showrunner. Start by watching how you relate to your body, breath and mind. If you need a gentle reminder, think of The Police. (The band, not the boys in blue.) Let their not-so-subtle, stalky lyrics serve as a mantra to begin the process of waking up: every move you make, every breath you take, watch yourself. Police yourself to release yourself, so you can stop sleepwalking and start living.

Key Takeaways

- You have to fight and take action in this lifetime, so may it be skilful, conscious action.
- Most of us don't take conscious action, but get caught up in activity and distraction.
- The world is stealing your energy, or 'prana', and it's up to you to wake up and reclaim it.
- Bring vitality to the vehicle you've been given – the body, mind and breath. Start by watching how you relate to them.

REFLECTION QUESTIONS

1. Do you ever have that experience of driving to a destination, but being so distracted that once you arrive, you can't remember how you got there? This week, notice those moments. Where do you tend to sleepwalk and not stay present?

2. Is there something you put off or procrastinate? Reflect on why. Then make a plan to combat it and take action.

3. How well are you nourishing yourself at the moment? Spend the next week monitoring how well you are doing with the physical layer – look at your sleep, hydration and

nutrition. Is there a habit that is potentially putting a hole in your petrol tank? Maybe you could get to bed an hour earlier, take a bottle of water with you all week or cut down on sugar. You know what the thing is! We all do. Get to it.

EXERCISE
THREE CONSCIOUS BREATHS

Breath meditation has its roots in Buddhism. It is said that it takes just a few conscious breaths to meditate. Thought leader Chade-Meng Tan takes it one step further. He teaches that the condition of the mind and body can be altered in one single breath. A conscious breath gives the mind a hook to practise taking a moment of mindful space, similar to what Pema Chodron calls a 'pause practice'. When the mind gets caught up in distracting thoughts, and our attention is being diverted all over the place, we pull it back into the present moment with breath. Vietnamese Zen master Thich Nhat Hanh suggests that breath meditation can magnify our focus and compassion, and awaken us to our true nature.

At the very least, it's a circuit-breaker to bring you into the present. So, let's put it to the test.

Wherever you are, find a comfortable seat. Bring your awareness into your physical body and notice the quality of your physical body. Notice the quality of your mind and your breath. Keeping the mouth closed, take a slow, deep, full inhale through both of your nostrils and open the mouth to exhale, letting the breath go. And then shift your awareness back to the body, the mind and breath. Notice if there is a change or not. Shift awareness back to the breath, and try three deep, conscious breaths. Keep the mind focused on the depth of these breaths. Take a deep, full inhale and a deep, slow exhale, opening the mouth to let it go. Once more, inhale through the nostrils, exhale to let the breath go. Once more, inhaling and exhaling. Return to breathing as normal, noticing the quality of the breath, the quality of your mind and the quality of your physical body. If this creates a shift for you, you can apply it to your daily life, simply taking a conscious full breath whenever needed.

CHAPTER 2

Slay the Energy Vampires

'An energy vampire is somebody
who literally zaps your energy dry.'

Judith Orloff

Multitasking: the Dis-Ease of Our Time

It's been proven that there are limits to how much the brain can handle and that multitasking is a myth. We know multitasking increases cortisol (the stress hormone) and adrenaline (the fight-or-flight hormone). It creates a dopamine addiction (the pleasure chemical), rewarding the brain for losing focus and searching for external stimulation. The prefrontal cortex, which is responsible for focusing your attention, has a magpie tendency to gravitate to bright, shiny new things (making you more distracted). Not only can multitasking reduce productivity, but it can be dangerous. One study found that emergency doctors who were dealing with multiple patients, nurses and paperwork at the same time made errors in prescriptions and left tasks unfinished.

And yet we revere multitasking as if it's something to aspire to. *How do they do it?* Well, actually, they don't. They make mistakes, have chronic fatigue, suffer from anxiety and take 689 vitamin supplements because they can't actually do it.

I mean, they try to. They give it a good nudge, like we all do. Keeping all the tabs open, all the time. Tabs open on our screens, in our lives, in our relationships, at home and at work. And we know what happens when we keep tabs open, don't we? We drain our battery. We know that, because the 12-year-old Apple Genius Bar guy scolded us about a lot of things at our last appointment, and that was one of them. But God forbid we close them. What if we need them open again in five minutes? Or five hours?

So, we keep them open in relationships. We Tinder and Bumble and Hinge, juggling several suitors at once. Even when we're in long-term relationships, or married, we 'chat harmlessly' to exes from our past. Because now we are only a click away from a version of ourselves who once upon a time had regrettable taste in plastic cat-eye frames, bandana midriff tops and men. Remember Fred, who you dated for like five minutes in 1999? Well, Fred remembers you. And now Fred can find you, in a matter of seconds, from the comfort of his smartphone. In the past, you wouldn't have heard from Fred again. You would have happily forgotten Fred existed. But we are no longer in 1999. And neither is Fred. We are in the abyss of a time where anyone can find you in a matter of clicks.

I dated someone a few years ago who was 'chatting harmlessly' to *several* (double digits) women online, after we'd been together for a year. When I brought it up with him, he explained that he just needed the validation. It's not that he didn't love me, he just needed the tabs open. Because we are *so* conditioned to keeping them open all the time. According to the American Academy of Matrimonial Lawyers, more than 80 per cent of US divorce attorneys have witnessed a rise in the number of divorces linked to social networking. Your Honour, I rest my case.

At work, we're physically present, sure. But we're checking Tinder and Insta, running our online business and getting ready for our Uber shift later. We're looking at Tripadvisor, planning the one week of joy we'll have to distract us from our otherwise restless lives (which will probably be cancelled due to a pandemic or work thing we can't get away from, let's be honest). We're working parents riddled with guilt, crying in the toilet at 11am on a Thursday because we missed our kid's first steps, but Sue from day care didn't – she sent us a video of the milestone moment. If we're not crying in the toilet, we're texting in there. Several studies revealed that an alarming number of us use the phone while on the toilet (80 per cent of men and 69 per cent of women according to one survey – and that's just the people who admit to doing it). We're here, we really are, but we're also miles away.

And then there's us in our cars. Conservative estimates suggest that more than half the population in Australia use smartphones while driving. A study by Virginia Tech Transportation Institute found that the risk of an accident increases sixfold when texting and twelvefold when dialling. I think we all know this. We know it's dangerous. And yet, we can't help it. We just can't wait until we're out of the car to check our news, socials and 63 different WhatsApp groups filled with memes of the moment.

Because our tabs are open all the time, we don't know how to close them anymore. We take melatonin, magnesium, CBD and sleepy tea to try and switch off at night. And, even then, we never really shut down properly. It's like 'sleep' mode on laptops – the computer brain isn't really getting deep rest, it's just hovering in some kind of in-between, not-on/not-off land. So, we never feel one hundred per cent rested and ready to restart the next day. But onwards we march.

The only time we ever allow that proper shut down to happen is when the system crashes and we burn out or get sick. Then there's no choice but to switch off, count to ten (minutes, hours, days or weeks, depending on how burnt out we are), reboot and restart. You have so much energy and so much time available to you in this precious lifetime. None of us knows how much or when it's going to run out, yet we keep all the tabs open, all the time, like we have an unlimited battery supply. They don't make modern devices like they used to. Those batteries don't last longer than a year or two. Tops. Let's stop treating our lives in the modern world like they are different.

Multitasking is not making your life *easier*. It's a disease. It brings *dis-ease* with what is. It keeps you tired, restless, powerless and distracted. And then you wonder why you are unable to do the important things – the things that count – like fighting the inevitable everyday battles of life.

If you want to find more inner strength, stop giving it away. Start noticing where your attention is going, then reclaim it and direct it where *you* choose, not what chooses you. It's really up to you. You can keep the tabs open and let them drain you dry, or you can close them and save your (battery) life.

Energy Vampires: Don't Invite Them In

There are some things in life that, no matter how much you put into them, you get nothing back from, apart from feeling depleted. Social media, toxic environments and 'those people' are the biggest culprits. They are energy drainers that will bleed you dry, vampire style.

Despite differing ideas about the mythology of vampires, there are some key characteristics we often see, such as their alluring charm and insatiable appetite. They're formidable because of their magnetic pull. It's one of the reasons we feel defenceless around them. But, the thing is, they have no power unless they're invited in. It's up to you to open the door and let them in.

Screen Vampires

Notice how you feel after you've lost yet another hour of your life to Instagram reels or getting triggered by that rabbit hole you went down reading posts of someone you have an aversion to. That hour you used on your phone scrolling, during a day where you didn't have time to exercise, meditate or call your grandma.

This is where discipline comes in (more on that later, too). Set yourself some limits (like so many of us do for our kids, just not for ourselves ... ahem) and stick to them. Get an alarm clock so you don't have your phone in the bedroom. Turn off notifications on your phone. Do whatever you can, but find a way to spend less time with the object that drains you dry.

When I think of the hours of my life that I've given away to true crime shows and mindless feel-good TV, I have to sometimes wonder ... I mean, I may be an expert in DNA analysis and criminal profiling but, seriously, surely with my limited energy as a working single parent, my time could be better spent elsewhere. We think 'zoning out' with screens is refuelling us. But it requires our attention, awareness and energy. On some level, it's actually depleting us. Now, that's not to say we can't binge-watch all our favourite shows. If it brings you pleasure, and doesn't leave you feeling more tired than when you started, what's the big deal? The deal is simply making those choices *consciously*. I know I'm tired and should be going to bed, rather than starting my fourth episode of *The Crown* tonight, but I'm making a conscious choice to watch the Queen's terrible parenting of Charles and deal with the consequences tomorrow at 6am when my alarm goes off. What can I say? Diana needs me.

Screens can be tricky. But what's even harder to manage is the energy-hijacking people in your life.

Hungry Ghosts

In Buddhism, there is a concept called 'hungry ghosts' – the ones whose desire can never be satiated. They may remind you of certain people in your life. You know, the friends and family where you just give, give, give and there's nothing in return? No energetic exchange. It's like an energetic bank account you just keep putting all your hard-earned energy into but you are never able to withdraw from. Somehow you're always in debt.

If you have energy vampires in your life, especially if you're an empath, people-pleaser or co-dependent (I already hear your familiar protests and excuses, because I know them well, I've used them all), setting boundaries and learning to say 'no' is not going to be easy. It's a skill that requires muscles you probably haven't used before. So, it might take a while to build that muscle. You won't like being the 'bad guy', and there will most likely be some discomfort as the relationship adjusts. It's hard to set a boundary in a place where there has not been one. I get that you're trying to be a 'good person'. I get that you don't want conflict. But, really, it's not up to anyone else to manage your energy. If you are willingly giving it away to someone who is happy to take it, then that is on you, not them.

Learn the power of 'no' and set good boundaries, even if it means letting go of some relationships (which will happen). Because if you don't, no amount of work trying to build your energy resources is going to matter. The hungry ghosts will consume everything in their path, leaving both your battery and their own running on empty.

Women's health expert Dr Christiane Northrup argues that energy vampires are a health risk because they create chronic stress, which in turn creates health problems in the immune, cardiovascular, neuroendocrine and central nervous systems that can manifest in autoimmune diseases, heart disease, obesity and depression. These people are making you sick. Stop letting them. Take your boundary vitamins, *Buffy-the-Vampire* slay them away and don't be fooled by how Edward-from-*Twilight* they are (all charming, brooding and sparkling in the sun). Put that garlic around your neck and get on with the business of living your life.

Guard your energy like your life depends on it. Because it does. The proof will be in how you feel long term as you fill up your tank and keep it full, without sneaky thieves drilling a hole in it and draining it all.

In summary: close the tabs, slay and restart your life.

Key Takeaways

- Multitasking is a myth. Don't buy into it.
- Close the tabs to save your (battery) life.
- Screens, people and places will steal your life force and, more often than not, give nothing back.
- Energy vampires are the hungry ghosts in your life who are never satiated and leave you feeling exhausted.
- It's up to you to set boundaries and learn the magic of 'no'.

REFLECTION QUESTIONS

1. Where do you leave tabs open in your life? Take a good look at why. And then get curious about what it feels like to close them. Focus on the one left open in front of you.

2. Make a list of the energy vampires in your life, from devices and social media to people or places.

3. How do these energy vampires make you feel?

4. Make a plan to set boundaries and then follow through like your life depends on it (because it does). E.g. phones away from 6pm, saying 'no' to someone you need to.

EXERCISE
BREATHING INTO THE BELLY

Setting boundaries and saying 'no' can create anxiety when we are not used to doing it. The third chakra (energy centre) around the navel is the seat of our ego and will. It's where we get our fire from. Whenever I feel anxious or not connected to my centre, I simply place my hands on the belly and take a few conscious breaths into the lower belly. It's a very quick way to trigger the parasympathetic nervous system (our rest-and-restore response that takes us out of the fight-or-flight response), while helping you come back to your centre, your strength and your ability to take action.

CHAPTER 3

Dharma: Purpose

'Your purpose in life is to find your purpose
and give your whole heart and soul to it.'

Buddha

One of the most important things you can do in this lifetime is discover who you are and why you are here. When you are connected to a deep sense of purpose, it's like you're plugged into a universal power source. You know you're connected to purpose when you lose track of time doing that thing and, unlike time spent with energy vampires, you never get tired. It's a miraculous kind of force you tap into. It's understandable then that there is a modern obsession with discovering your purpose, or *raison d'être* as the French so aptly put it.

The desire to understand one's purpose is not a new concept. It's something we've pondered as humans since the beginning of time. It's very valuable in terms of providing motivation, drive and goals. The *Gita* is filled with rich symbolism, including our warrior, Arjuna, with his bow and arrow. Just like Arjuna, we are all warriors on the battlefield of life, equipped with our own bow and arrows. Having a target to aim each arrow at fosters satisfaction and helps us focus. Otherwise, we are carelessly shooting our arrows around, in the form of thoughts, words and actions. Who knows where they may land, or who they might hurt. If we have to take action, may we be the archers of the world. Taking some time in life to be still, in introspection, pulling the arrow of intention into the bow in order to get clarity about what we want to do with this precious life we've been given. Then we focus, mindfully, and project that outwards with our might and vigour. This is how we start to live our lives on purpose, propelled by our inner power.

But modern Western culture has peddled a misbelief that everything we do must be filled with meaning, otherwise it's a waste of time. If it doesn't have 'impact', we feel it's pointless. As though the mundane, day-to-day experiences have nothing to offer us in the way of satisfaction. But the reality is, that's all we really have – the everyday moments. They're so much of our life and experience, and yet we pass them by, waiting for ... um ... we're not really sure what. But whatever it is, it has to have 'impact'!

It's a misconception to think meaning and purpose only exist in big, grand-gesture displays. If we can't learn to find contentment and joy in the tiny moments, life will be very disappointing.

One of the main themes of the *Gita* is *dharma*, which can be translated as purpose. My friend Noelle, who is the living embodiment of yoga, speaks about dharma as 'something that can't be taken away from you'. I love this idea. It's that indescribable thing that lives in you and lights you up. That 'spark'. This is something that no pandemic, no illness, no bushfire, no GFC, no break-up, no divorce and no battlefield can take away from you.

Your Spark

Disney, George Lucas and in fact much of Hollywood owe a lot of royalties to ancient philosophy. *Star Wars*? Yoga (YoDa? Hello!?). *Avatar*? The *Bhagavad Gita*. *Frozen*? We'll get to that one.

One of my favourite movies that explores the idea of dharma is Pixar's *Soul*. (Spoiler alert: if you haven't seen it, stop reading now and watch it – it's delightful). In *Soul*, our protagonist, Joe, is helping 22, who is 'sparkless', find her spark. Joe, like all humans, thinks his spark is his purpose. An accomplished and passionate jazz pianist, he assumes his spark, and therefore purpose, is to play piano. It's what takes him into that elusive state – let's call it a 'flow state' – where everything disappears, including time, and all you feel is deep immersion and connectivity to something greater than yourself. As 22 experiences life on Earth for the first time, trying to find her spark, Joe witnesses what it's like to see the world as a child again through new eyes. He reflects on all the moments in his life that made him feel whole, satisfied and loved. The moments imbued with meaning and joy. Eventually, he comes to realise that his spark exists in everyday moments – his mum bathing him as a kid, his dad playing piano with him, riding his bike, looking up at the sky, seeing sunlight stream through autumn leaves. He understands that a 'spark' isn't a soul's purpose. Rather, it's just a sign that they're ready to live life on Earth.

Are you ready to live your life on Earth? This one incredible chance you've been given? Don't waste it, wishing it away, waiting to get to the end game or the big, 'meaningful' moment. What if the end game is this moment? But you miss it, because you're waiting for something that may never come? You, sitting here, reading this book, wherever you are. Can this be enough? Because that is where your access to real power lies. Making 'impact' in the tiny moments.

Don't miss your spark. Don't miss the moments of meaning. Don't miss your life. Everyone whose kids are all grown up will go on about this when you have little ones. 'Don't wish it away. Don't be in a rush for the next stage. One day, you'll look at them and they're suddenly teenagers.' But none of us really listens. We're too tired.

There were so many challenges in those early days of motherhood. The sleepless nights, the nappies, the teething, the fevers, the sickness. It took until Gabriel was three before I woke up.

I remember it vividly. We were at our family farm in the country, all rugged up to go for a walk. He insisted on wearing his Batman gear, as always. An autumn afternoon, the leaves were orangey-gold, the sky was pink and my masked superhero was squeezing my hand in little, woollen Batman gloves. We wandered along muddy paths surrounded by an only-in-the-country sense of quiet. It was one of those deeply spiritual moments of connectivity and love. I exhaled, expanded and felt it all. After three minutes, the machine-gun questions came, as did the complaining and the 'carry me'. I felt myself contract, I felt my frustration rise, but I stopped. I picked him up, smelt his hair, listened to all the questions and kissed his masked face. Because I knew time was racing. We wouldn't get this moment again. And it was hard to imagine, but I knew, deep in my bones, that one day soon he would not want to wear his Batman gear on our walk in the country. He would not want me to carry him. He would not want to hold my hand. He would not have 593 questions about everything. He would not drop his skanky plastic legless dinosaur (found in the mud at the park last week) and we wouldn't have to retrace all our steps to find it (even though we were almost home). It was hard to imagine, but I knew it was coming. So, I walked with Batman. I scooped him up and stole my cuddles. I answered all the questions and searched for lost dinosaurs.

This was not the grand, exciting life of meaning and creating impact I'd planned or imagined. This was very different. But it felt deeper, more profound, like I was connected to everything. It felt ... like love. It felt like home. I'm filled with gratitude for these fleeting golden moments. These fragments of nostalgia that will slip away with the autumn leaves. We spend our lives panning for gold and yet, here it is. Before our very eyes. Walking in the countryside with Batman. Blink, and you'll miss it.

He's eight years old now. He still holds my hand every now and then. He still wants to hang out with me (mostly). Every time he leans in for a cuddle, every time he holds my hand, every time he gets into my bed and says, 'Morning, Mum', I try to wake up. I don't want to miss any more moments. Because our moments together ... they're my spark.

Don't Find Your Purpose; Live Your Life on Purpose

Many people don't have the privilege to contemplate what their purpose is or what they should be doing with their lives. The luxury of doing so is based on things that are out of our control, such as what situation we are born into. For those of us lucky enough to do so – to discover what lights us up, what we believe in and want to fight for – that is a gift to be grateful for.

But even if we are not in that position or we don't know what our dharma is, we can all live our lives on purpose. Intentionally being present in every mundane moment and staying awake is enough. It's a lot. It's a miracle, when you think about it.

My friend Phil describes dharma as doing a whole bunch of things that are *not* your purpose, in order to discover what *is* your purpose. I love this perspective, that the process of discovery holds just as much value as the result. That you don't necessarily wake up one day knowing what it is you're meant to do. That it's valuable to try things that are not your dharma, as it may be the only way you work out what is. Nothing you do is a waste of time. No job, project, love affair, friendship, marriage – it's all part of you finding your way. Discovering what is for you by first understanding what is not for you. Stop beating yourself up over what's happened in the past. Be grateful for the lessons and move on.

I hope this liberates you from feeling that if you haven't found your purpose, there's something wrong with you. You can be connected to dharma in the minuscule, always. You can be connected to it in your home, with your family, on dates, doing that job you don't love – you can choose to stay awake and connect to some part of the experience. I hope it is comforting to realise that we don't have to have some big dream or goal we are chasing to be centred in our soul's work. Your spark is always with you. No one can take it away from you. You just have to stay awake so you don't miss it. Then, like Joe in *Soul*, you are ready to live your life on Earth.

Key Takeaways

- It's important to find your purpose in life, but it's just as valuable to discover meaning in the everyday moments.
- Your 'spark', that thing that ignites you, can't be taken away from you.
- Live your life on purpose, instead of searching for purpose.

REFLECTION QUESTIONS

1. Reflect on moments in your life when you've felt truly happy and connected. Can you identify your spark?

2. What are the tasks that you can do for hours and never feel tired?

3. When you contemplate the idea of your life's purpose or the greater meaning of your life, what comes up for you? Certainty? Fear? Confusion?

Journal your reflections. This is where we can start to understand our purpose.

EXERCISE
MINDFUL WALKING

Studies have found that a sense of purpose in life is positively influenced by a meditative practice. Mindful walking is a great way to meditate, especially if you find it challenging to sit. You can do it anywhere, anytime, even walking to the car park or across town.

It's a great opportunity to connect to the world around you. The unification of the body and breath, while experiencing the world as you move through it, brings you into the present. Linking your breath to the steps you take helps you become aware of the wholeness of the moment, according to Vietnamese Zen master Thich Nhat Hanh.

While there is no one way to mindfully walk, here are some practical tools to try:

- Get curious. As you walk, notice the way your body moves – your posture, the way your feet connect to the earth, your body weight, which muscles you're using, your arms swinging alongside the body.
- Become aware of your surroundings with curiosity. What can you see and feel in the world around you?

What are the colours and textures? Is there a breeze?
Can you feel the warmth of the sun? What can you
smell, hear, maybe even touch, as you pass by?
Take it all in.

- Now, watch your breath. Allow it to move naturally
with your walking rhythm, ensuring it is easeful and
deep. Watch how the breath flows and changes.
Notice the mind wandering, acknowledge where it
has gone and come back to the breath.

CHAPTER 4

Duty

'Fulfil all your duties.

Action is better than inaction.'

Bhagavad Gita 3:8 (translated by Eknath Easwaran)

We all have moments in life where our purpose becomes crystal clear. Sometimes you listen to it, and other times you don't. Those times that you do pay attention – perhaps set goals, work hard, make huge sacrifices and focus with determination – may pay off. But it's not guaranteed. Even if you've said your affirmations every day and done all the manifestation courses under the sun, sometimes things just don't work out. Perhaps you had a responsibility that took you away, obstacles you couldn't overcome, or things just fell apart (as they do).

Life Happens While You Are Making Other Plans

While we are trying to succeed in achieving our goals, life has other plans. Life is not interested in your success. It is interested in your growth. So, it's going to give you experiences to facilitate that growth. It wants you to understand who you are beyond your external circumstances, your personality and your best-laid plans. Because on the other side of your limited perceptions, that's where your true strength lies.

Life wants you to discover you are powerful, vast and limitless. That all the monuments you believe define you are actually sandcastles that can be washed away. So, it's going to put you in situations that can teach you who, and what, you really are. By showing you who, and what, you are not. If you're interested in fulfilling your immeasurable potential, whatever you think you are is going to be stripped away. (We will look at this more in Chapter 6.)

When You Don't Choose the Battlefield

One of the tricky things about the fact that life involves taking conscious action, that you have to fight, is that often you don't get to choose the battlefield.

In the *Gita*, dharma is often translated as purpose, as we've discussed. But Sanskrit is an incredibly rich and complex language – each syllable and word has multiple meanings – so dharma can also be translated as 'duty'. This is where I think the idea of finding our purpose gets very interesting – when we don't get to choose. Sometimes our purpose is an obligation or responsibility. Something we have to do. It's a call to action on a battlefield we didn't plan for or anticipate. And our resistance to stepping onto it, while yearning to be somewhere else we *think* will give us greater meaning, is inevitably going to cause pain.

I have a friend who *really* wanted a family. She believed her purpose in life was to be a mum. She spent much of her thirties in a relationship with a man who kept assuring her they would start a family 'one day'. As she was faced with the cruel joke that is the female body clock, the reality of 'one day' became now. With a physiological ultimatum, her partner realised he didn't want a family after all. She still loved him, but she loved her unborn kids more, so she made the tough decision to leave. The grace she left him with, no blame, no shame, (just good old-fashioned diving into online dating like there's no tomorrow), was impressive to witness. She made Tinder look fun. She just got on with her new life. Because of this, she met a bunch of great guys and was having a blast, but then she found herself unexpectedly on a new battlefield. The battlefield of ageing parents. Both of her parents got sick, very sick, at once. As an only child, she chose to step up and take care of them. She knew these were her final years to meet a partner to potentially have a family with. But she also knew it was the final chapter she had with her parents. When I asked her how she felt about it all, the acceptance and grace she displayed was awe-inspiring. There was no drama, no torture, no doubt. 'They're my parents. They brought me into this world. They gave me everything I have. I want to honour them by taking care of them when they need me the most,' she said.

Your Moral Compass

That's it, I thought. *That's what the* Gita *is talking about*. She had a massive job on her hands, it was hard work and I know she had moments of grief and despair. It wasn't what she'd planned for this chapter of her life. But she knew in her bones she was doing the right thing, and *that* gave her the strength to do what must be done.

I know so many incredible people who have given up everything to be there for family and friends in times of need. Or friends who are activists that got very clear about what they believed in, and what they wanted to fight for, and put their own lives on the line for the freedom and rights of others.

When we know deep down we are doing the right thing, when we are being navigated across choppy seas by our moral compass, we can't go wrong. We can't go off course. We can't be shipwrecked. Somehow, we find the strength to cross any sea, come what may.

Accepting Your Duty

In the bleak trenches of the newborn bubble, I grieved the life I lost and the part of me that didn't exist anymore. The one who was always laughing, creating and connecting with her crew. The one who travelled, performed and drank whisky with her sister. The one who devoured literature, movies, theatre and art. She was gone. Replaced with someone I couldn't recognise. Someone lonely, hopeless and fearful. I remember one morning, as I was sitting (drinking tea, not whisky) with my sister, I suddenly started belly-laughing as baby G pulled a funny face while looking at a picture of a deer on my coffee mug. My sister remarked that she hadn't heard me laugh in a long time. At that moment, something shifted. It was time to wake up. I needed to find those moments whenever I could – to attain joy in what was – and step into my new life completely with as much presence and enthusiasm as I could muster. It didn't happen overnight ... but as I yielded to my duty as a single mum, and ceased wishing life to be anything other than what it was, everything became a little more easeful. There is great strength in accepting duty, accepting the battlefield you are on and letting go of what cannot be.

Service

Dharma isn't asking you to change the world. It's asking you to be of service in *your* world, to follow your moral compass and to recognise that sometimes our purpose is a duty, something that must be done, whether we like it or not. It's asking you to pay attention and find your spark in the tiny, no matter what circumstance you find yourself in.

Somewhere along the way, success got mixed up with fame and celebrity. Fame obsession and visibility wasn't a thing when I was growing up. There were no influencers. We had the supermodels to ogle at – fierce Naomi, classy yoga-head Christy and quirky Linda. We thought they were cool, but we didn't want to be them. They weren't accessible to us. They were goddesses residing on some heavenly supermodel planet somewhere (well, Kate Moss was on planet Calvin Klein). But their lives were not for us to aspire to. So, when did it all change? When did we start valuing people for their likes, visibility and popularity? For their (apparent) wealth and power? For their 'reach'? Fame has become a currency. An economy. These things are not bad, though. Money gives us freedom. Empowerment is liberating. Building a community is a gift. Skilful leaders have the ability to change the world, to take great action and really live their purpose.

But, let's not confuse living our purpose, or success, with fame and followers. Let's not confuse being of great service to the world with visibility. Live your purpose by being of value to your community, by the quality of your relationships – by being a present parent, loyal friend, collaborative colleague, loving child, committed partner, inspiring boss, generous customer, planet caretaker. Live your purpose in your home life, at work, as you buy bread. That is the currency of true success. That is how you change the world. By being of service to those around you.

You Can Change Your Path

There's nothing to say that you have to figure out your purpose, choose a path and then stay on it forever. You can change your path. I hope you do. I hope you get to reinvent yourself a million times over. I hope

you discover that unique thing that no one else can do quite like you.
I hope you get fired up about changing the world and then use your
precious life force to do so.

But if you find yourself on the wrong path, it doesn't mean you have
to keep going in that direction. Hell no. Don't waste your life. Take a
moment to pause and get back on track.

I'm not good with geography, maps, navigation and whatnot. Let's say
it's not my forte. My yoga teacher David Life talks about your path
not being fixed in terms of going in the wrong direction on a freeway.
You can always get back on track and head in another direction. It just
requires some conscious action.

When I lived in Los Angeles, I avoided the freeways like the plague.
I hated that moment when I had to take my little red 1980s convertible
Ford Mustang from the turnoff onto the freeway and try to hit
the speed limit with all the oversized SUVs tearing past me. Now,
hypothetically, if I was going in the wrong direction (yes, it happened
more than once), what should I do? If I realised that I was heading
south to San Diego when I should have been heading north to Santa
Barbara, what would happen if I just slammed on the brakes? It would
be a disaster and I would undoubtedly create a lot of carnage, with
many casualties, including me. This is what can happen when we are

on the battlefield of life and we decide we don't want to fight. When we realise that we are not living our purpose or we are faced with an obligation or duty we don't want to do. So, we give up, check out or throw our toys out of the cot.

You can change direction, for sure. But it requires patience, planning, attention and regrouping before you get back on track. You have to indicate, get off the freeway, look at the GPS, figure out where you went wrong, where you want to go and then head in the right direction. This is why Elizabeth Gilbert in her book *Big Magic* says it's not a great idea to decide you're going to be a writer and quit your day job. You can't be creative if you're worrying about how you're going to survive. You can change your life, but you need to get off the freeway first.

I used to spend quite a bit of time in remote Northern Territory. I worked on a project there for a few years – a series of residencies aimed at engaging young people in storytelling and writing a play about what life was like for these kids in remote Australia. It became a second home and I formed an extraordinary bond with the country and communities. One trip, in the middle of the 'build-up' (peak summer heat before the rain kicks in), a friend came to stay with me. I wanted to take her to the arts centre in Beswick, a community I'd been to a number of times. We were doing our best *Thelma-&-Louise* road trip, rocking out some excellent car singing, solving the world's problems (and talking about boys) as I drove on autopilot. It took a while for me to realise I'd missed the turn-off and we were well and truly on our way to Alice Springs. Now, this would have been fine, except I'd banked on heading straight to Beswick, so I didn't fill up the petrol tank when I had the chance to back in town. I tried to do the calculations. We could head back to town, but I wasn't sure we'd make it. At least if the car died on the way back, though, we'd be more likely to see other cars. I'd arranged for someone to meet us at the arts centre to let us in, but with no phone reception, there was no way of contacting them or anyone else. I figured we could try to make it to Beswick and, if we did, we'd just have to get someone from town to drive some petrol out to us (not sure who that would be ...). But, if we didn't make it, there was less likelihood of any cars coming past for some time. With an almost empty fuel tank, surrounded by dry communities with no petrol on a scorching-hot day with no water, phone or GPS, it was one of those city-girl rookie-error moments. We took a calculated risk, headed towards Beswick, didn't make it, but *did* make it – with the petrol light on – to Barunga, another remote community that was on the way. Doing my best damsel in distress, I managed to convince the local council guy to give us some lawnmower fuel, which he wasn't sure would work in a car but was willing to let us give a red-hot go. As luck would have it, it did work and we had just enough to make it back to town. The rental car survived (as far as I know) and so did we.

You can plan your journey with the best of intentions. You can use your moral compass to guide you. You can enjoy the ride like Thelma and Louise. But, sometimes, you need to change your course. You need to pause, regroup, re-imagine, replan, refuel and reboot. Otherwise, you'll end up lost, out of fuel or driving off the Grand Canyon in a 1966 Thunderbird.

Your purpose isn't some fixed thing, so you needn't get fixed on it. Better to be fixed on being in your life completely, so you don't miss a thing. So you don't wake up asking, 'How the hell did I get here?' So you can get back on track, living your life with proper petrol in the tank instead of lawnmower fuel.

Key Takeaways

- Sometimes life happens while you are making other plans and your duty becomes your purpose. You don't always get to choose the battlefield.
- When you're guided by your moral compass, you can't go wrong.
- There is strength in yielding to our duty and letting go of wishing things to be other than they are.
- Purpose and success are about service, not celebrity.
- Your dharma isn't fixed. You can change your path.

REFLECTION QUESTIONS

1. In what places do you resist your dharma? Is there somewhere you find yourself 'phoning it in' and not giving your full presence and attention? How does it make you feel? How can you bring more joy and acceptance to that place?

2. Where are the places you feel of service in your life? Family? Friends? Community? How does it make you feel when you contribute to them?

3. Where do you feel stuck? Is there action you can take to get unstuck?

4. Do you feel like you are on the right path? If not, what does the right path look like? How will it feel to be on it?

EXERCISE
'I SURRENDER' MEDITATION

This meditation is especially useful when we find ourselves in circumstances beyond our control.

Choose a comfortable seat. Sit in a relaxed state with the spine upright, supporting your back if you need. Close your eyes. Bring awareness into your physical body and notice the quality of your physical body. How does the body feel? Notice the quality of the mind. Notice the quality of your breath. Imagine there is a piece of string at the top of your head that lifts you taller, creating space between the vertebrae. Consciously relax your shoulders down, relax the forehead, jaw and throat. Be still – this is the tricky part. Commit to stillness for this brief time. Notice the breath in and out through the nostrils. Don't modify the breath in any way, just allow it to move freely and naturally. Notice cool air moving in, warmer air moving out. As you notice the inhale, think of the word 'I' and as you exhale, the word 'surrender'. Inhaling 'I', exhaling 'surrender'. The mind will wander – notice where the mind has wandered and come back to the breath. Inhaling 'I' and exhaling 'surrender'. 'I surrender'. Bring your awareness back to the breath, allow the mantra to drop away. Notice the quality of the breath, the quality of the physical body and the quality of the mind. Take a deep, slow inhale and exhale to let the breath go.

CHAPTER 5

Make a Mess of It

'It is better to do your own duty badly

than to perfectly do another's.'

Bhagavad Gita 3:35 and 18:47 (translated by Stephen Mitchell)

I've always loved stories. Some of my most vivid memories as a child were those of books and movies. I remember reading *The Hobbit* on the couch in the sun and walking into the car park after watching *E.T.* with Mum, sobbing: 'It's not fair!' I love how stories help us feel and understand the world. So, it's no surprise to me that every time I veer off the path of storytelling, I'm swiftly pulled back on. Whatever work it is I'm doing, storytelling will sneak its way into the process, and if it has no place there, then I don't often stay long.

When it comes to career, many of us have made choices along the way out of expectation. The expectations of both ourselves and others. We feel pressure to live a certain way or follow a particular path – maybe because we're really good at something, it will make our family happy or it cultivates a feeling of worthiness in some way.

Whatever the case, when you follow a path that doesn't belong to you, it feels like you're wearing an ill-fitting costume. No matter how successful you are or how many accolades you receive, you'll feel like an imposter, and there will be a sense of emptiness and restlessness. Like that feeling when you turn up to an appointment and you realise that you're at the wrong address. The pervading sense of *I don't belong here* will follow you wherever you go, casting a shadow over any light that the path you're on provides.

There's a reason they say, 'Do something you're passionate about, and you'll never work a day in your life.' Because when you are on your path, no matter the obstacles, no matter the challenges, you're connected to your soul and receive unlimited energy. You feel a sense of belonging, no matter how hard things get, and the costume fits perfectly.

When I taught kids acting classes, I had many parents come to me for advice. They wanted to know if their kid was 'good enough', whether they should waste their time getting into a career where success, from a material perspective, is as elusive as winning the lottery. Should they encourage them to do something else, such as a university degree? I had to explain to them time and time again that if their kid is creative, if they have the acting bug, it doesn't matter what they do or say, now or in the future. It'll follow them and they'll follow it.

I did an economics degree at university. I loved it and I tried hard to make it work in the corporate world, but my body was covered in psoriasis, I was miserable and I always felt restless. Creativity, and storytelling, specifically, is an integral part of how I exist in the world. It chose me. Of that, I have no doubt. Maybe you haven't picked up a paintbrush or guitar or put on a pair of ballet shoes for decades, but that part of you is always there. Maybe you don't actually paint anymore, but that part of you plays out in your passion for baking and your creative approach to team-building at work.

It's not to say we all have to be artists. We definitely don't. The world needs all the glorious, creative, kind and strong people to be in other vocations, too. Life happens, and paying bills means creative pursuits have to be balanced with responsibilities.

It's your job to weigh up all the practical realities of modern life, get very clear on your values and purpose, and then operate from that place. There's no one way to do life. But as long as you do it (as Ol' Blue Eyes Frank Sinatra sang so eloquently) your way, you can't go wrong. Sure, you'll make mistakes and run into obstacles like all of us, but you'll always find the strength to do what you need to do. It's when we are living for others, trying to follow a path that is not actually ours, that we get into trouble and feel like we can't go on.

Don't live someone else's life. Don't put someone else's costume on (gross). It will never fit. Don't live a version of your life you had pictured, wanted and fought for but that just doesn't exist anymore. Make a big fat mess of your own life, but make it yours. You'll learn more from your failures on your own imperfect path than you ever will from your wins on a road that's not for you.

It's Never Too Late – Lessons from the Virabhadra Story

Some of the most recognisable *asana* (physical postures) in yoga are the warrior poses. Called *virabhadrasana* in Sanskrit, they relate to the mythology of a specific fierce warrior called Virabhadra. The story of Virabhadra is one of my favourites because it's a love story and it reminds us that it's never too late.

As all good old love stories go, it begins when boy meets girl. But this was not just any boy and girl. This was a young, charismatic rock-God called Shiva and a gentle, kind and loving beauty named Sati. And, of course, as young, foolish people do, they fell in love.

Now, Sati's dad, Daksha, didn't like Shiva at all. I mean, he's not exactly the guy you bring home to meet the parents. He was a yogi, for goodness' sake, who had dreads, hung out in cemeteries, sang, danced, wore a snake around his neck and was known to have an epic temper. He even chopped one of his creator's heads off in a rage. Unfortunately, his creator just happened to be Sati's grandfather. Awkward. Cutting your future grandpa-in-law's head off is not the way to the in-laws' hearts. Amiright?

Despite her dad's protests, Sati dug her heels in and stood by Shiva. She recognised that we all make mistakes and it's never too late to change. And so, she married him.

In response, in true stubborn father-in-law style, Daksha threw a big party and, like a petulant teenager, invited everyone in the universe except Sati and Shiva. Sati arrived at the party to confront her dad, but we all know how it rolls when you try to educate your parents about ... well ... anything. So, he got all De-Niro-in-*Meet-the-Parents*, she cried, then did what we all wish we could do when our parents trigger us ... she meditated until she self-immolated.

Shiva was obviously not happy to hear that the love of his life had burst into flames, so he pulled one of his dreads out, threw it on the ground and created a fierce warrior called Virabhadra to avenge her death. Virabhadra broke through the ground, brandishing his sword, raced to the party and chopped Daksha's head off. Shiva followed shortly after, discovering what Virabhadra had done and felt a bit shit. There were no winners here, and he knew Sati wouldn't be thrilled to know he'd decapitated her dad. He tried to find Daksha's head but, unable to locate it, he found an excellent goat's head to replace it with instead.

And they all lived happily ever after.

Shiva represents our 'higher selves'. The 'good' you. The 'you' when you're calm, steady, conscious, patient, reasonable and well slept. Daksha represents our ego – our rightness, judgements and fixed sense of the world. But, notice in the story that even Shiva gets it wrong. Even the 'good you' makes mistakes. Even the 'good you' has a little Virabhadra.

We all know those moments of chopping people's heads off. Swinging our swords fuelled by anger or fear, or because we feel we are 'right'. Sometimes, we believe it's for very good reason. Someone we love may have been hurt and we want to avenge them. A boundary may have been crossed and we don't know how to set one kindly. So, we brandish our sword and swing it around. But, sometimes, we chop the wrong person's head off. Or we're just shadow-boxing with our swords, waving them around, hoping we'll hit something or someone that'll make us feel better. Sometimes, without knowing why or how, we just mess up.

There's no point in beating ourselves up because we got it wrong. We all make mistakes. We all do stupid things. (Especially for love.) Things that seem perfectly reasonable at the time. You and I and everyone else – that's the deal of being human. Even your best self will mess up. You will brandish your sword in an unguarded moment. You'll scream at the kids, burn all your bridges and throw your toys out of the cot. You'll fight with your mum, back the wrong man and lose it all in a bet. You'll be in a job that's killing you, send that 'let-me-tell-you-a-thing-or two' text and cut off your nose to spite your face.

But ... it's never too late. To stop, make amends, start again, change, move on, set a boundary, say you're sorry, let it go, choose love, forgive and learn from your mistakes.

That's where your real strength lies. Not in your sword. Not in your brazen reactivity. But in your capacity to forgive yourself, and others, for making mistakes. Allow those experiences to humble instead of harden you, to burn away your old patterns instead of burning bridges and to widen your circle of compassion instead of imprisoning you in rigidity and dogma. Stop the blame and shame, the self-flagellation and regret. Pick yourself up, make it right and start again. Because it's never too late to find a goat's head. (PS: No goats were harmed in the telling of this story.)

Key Takeaways

- When you're walking someone else's path, you'll feel like an imposter – like you're wearing an ill-fitting costume.
- Live your own life completely. Make a mess of it, but make it yours.
- We're all going to make mistakes. It's never too late to forgive or find a goat's head.

REFLECTION QUESTIONS

1. Is there an area of your life where you feel like you're living for others or walking their path?

2. Is there somewhere in your life you feel like you've 'messed up'? What are the feelings that arise from this perspective?

3. List all the things you learned in the process. Then write a letter to yourself, forgiving yourself, and sending gratitude for all you learned in the process.

4. Write a letter to someone you may have caused harm to in an unconscious moment. You don't need to send it, unless you feel compelled to.

EXERCISE
GRATITUDE MEDITATION

A growing body of research has shown that the conscious practice of gratitude has enormous benefits, including decreased levels of depression, higher levels of wellbeing, trust in strangers and increased sleep quality. In this gratitude meditation, you practise cultivating gratitude for the times you messed up.

Choose a comfortable seat or lie down on your back. Take a moment to bring your awareness to your physical body, noticing the quality of your body, mind and breath.

Shift your awareness back to your physical body, to the space around the heart. Notice how it feels. What sensations are there? Shift your focus to the breath. Watch the inhale and the exhale. Bring into your mind someone you may have caused harm to, intentionally or not. As you inhale, think of the word 'gratitude'. As you exhale, think of the name or face of someone you may have caused harm to and send them thanks for all you learned in the process. See them as happy and free. Hold them in your heart space. Continue to inhale gratitude and exhale their name or face, until you're ready to move on to someone else. When you are finished, when no one else comes to mind, send love and forgiveness to yourself and hold yourself in your heart space. Feel gratitude for all you have learned. Then, let go of the gratitude practice. Notice your breath. Shift all of your awareness back into the heart space. How does it feel? Take a slow inhale, and a slow exhale to let the breath go.

CHAPTER 6

When You Lose Your Superpowers

'To know what you are, you must first
investigate and know what you are not.'
Shri Nisargadatta Maharaj

We all have a superpower. That thing that makes you uniquely you.
It's often easier to identify it in others. You know that friend who, no
matter what is going on in your life, always manages to make things
feel bearable? Or the person who is really good at bringing people
together, creating communities and bridging gaps? Maybe it's someone
in the corporate world who slays when it comes to negotiating, or that
manager who can unite a team like no one else?

My friend Jade is a traditional Chinese medicine ninja who eases the
suffering of so many who have exhausted every other path. Everyone
who comes into contact with her will testify to her magic hands and
Jedi ways. My sister's brain is her superpower. Her capacity to analyse,
comprehend and communicate reams of complex information in a
simple way, whether in her past career as a journo or her current foray
into medicine, is unmatched. My friend Lucie has this genuinely
positive outlook on life, where her glass is always half full. She sees the
good in everyone and everything. She makes a shitty job or situation
look fun and fabulous. In my early days of parenting, she was the one
turning up at my house, making me brush my hair and put clothes
on, insisting we leave the compound for coffee. She has this knack for
validating your suffering and, at the same time, making you feel like
everything will be A-okay. My friend Christian makes people feel like
they can do anything. He's inspiring and people are drawn to him,
so he books out workshops, classes and retreats. He's not reinventing

the wheel in terms of what he offers – in fact, there are many others who are more skilled than him. But his passion, and ability to make everyone around him feel happy and invincible, means people just don't care. They choose him. He genuinely wants to empower everyone he comes into contact with. He doesn't judge, he doesn't get dogmatic, he just makes people feel good.

There's nothing wrong with having superpowers – they can be very beneficial to those around you. The problem is that we rely on them and spend our lives reinforcing them, which makes us forget who we really are and where our true power lies.

Not Knowing Who You Really Are

The date is disputed, but somewhere between the 5th century BCE and 4th century CE, the great sage Patanjali wrote the *Yoga Sutras*, one of the foundational texts of classical yoga philosophy. In his book, he describes the key barriers called '*kleshas*' or 'afflictions' that prevent you from seeing clearly. They are obstacles to peace in your life and, ultimately, they will hinder your ability to access your true power.

The first one is a lack of knowledge of who you really are. It is the misbelief that you are just your body, mind, breath and personality. On one level, you are those things. As humans living an embodied

experience, it's natural to put the costume of the self on. As Tay Tay
will attest, there's only ever going to be one of you. The whole point
is to have fun with that. So, it's natural that you spend a lot of time
fortifying that 'you-ness'. But this reinforcement of your 'you-ness'
requires a lot of energy.

On another level, there is a part of you that is beyond all that. It doesn't
care about the personality part of the self. It's more interested in what
sits underneath. It's plugged into something universal and limitless.
It's what resides in the depths of your soul. Access that, and you'll have
inner strength on tap. The thing is, we don't really prioritise connecting
with that part of ourselves. We're too busy reinforcing our individuality.
And connecting with the universal part of self requires stillness, faith
and doing things that can feel like an indulgence in our busy lives.

But if you want freedom and inner strength, there is no other choice.
You have to understand who you are. Beyond your 'you-ness'. Another
way is to simply notice how quickly you go into 'my'. Jon Kabat-Zinn
says this is one of the key practices of mindfulness. Seeing how we jump
to our 'my-ness' all the time – my job, my life, my kids, my money, and
on it goes. The thing is, all of those can be taken away from you but, like
your spark, real knowledge of who you are, the part of you connected to
everything else in the universe, cannot be. It's like a flame that no one,
and nothing, can extinguish.

So, find ways to connect with that flame. Sit. Be still. Meditate. Contemplate. Lie on the grass. Float in the ocean. Watch your breath. Listen to the world around you. Do what you need to feel connected inside, not out. Once you do, you'll be more powerful than any superhero.

Putting on the Costume and Believing You're Batman

My son Gabriel used to love dress-ups. We went through a proper superhero phase that lasted for what felt like eternity. Every day, before we left the house, he would put on his costume, which was often a melange of superheros: Batman mask, Superman top, Iron Man pants and Thanos' glove. Off we'd go to do our daily chores. There was always someone, from a friendly shop assistant to a well-meaning person on the street, who would say: 'Hello Batman!' Razor-fast, not missing a beat, he would promptly reply with a deadpan face: 'I'm not Batman.' Because, you see, he wasn't confused. We are the ones who are confused.

We play dress-ups by putting on the costume of ourselves and then spending a lot of time and energy convincing everyone around us 'we're Batman'. I'm Rachael! Look at my Rachael-ness. All this time and energy is spent trying to convince everyone you are something you are not. No wonder you are exhausted.

Because of this misunderstanding that you are just the superhero outfit you wear, you get stuck in the ego and attach to your costume. You'll experience it in everyday life by waiting your turn to speak instead of listening, wanting people to know who you are and what you believe in and in your need to be right.

There's nothing wrong with getting clear about your value system and holding to your moral code. There's nothing wrong with enjoying your life and becoming a good person, like Luke Skywalker choosing the path of the Jedi. But why, oh why, do we need everyone to know about it? Why do we need to be right? Why do we need people to know who we *think* we are? Because the ego is fighting for its life. It doesn't want you to know that you'll be fine if you take off your costume. That no one really cares what you believe in or what costume you're wearing – because they're clinging for dear life to their own costumes, trying to convince everyone that 'they're Batman!' The ego doesn't want you to know that you are enough. That underneath your rightness is nothing and everything. That you are the limitless ocean of awareness. No, the ego doesn't want you to know about that. It would drown there. So, it creates separation. Between you and me, us and them, right and wrong.

It requires so much energy to pretend you are someone you are not. It's way more liberating to play dress-ups, put your costume on and have fun in your 'you-ness'. To enjoy your superpowers. But to understand on some level that it's all just make-believe – one big, glorious act – so we might as well start playing. We might as well start relishing the crazy ride that is our lives. We might as well enjoy the show.

Don't be limited by this experience of just being you. Do what you can to feel the dichotomy that you are your unique self, yes, but you are also limitless.

Allow that understanding to liberate those around you. Let them dress up as whatever superhero they want to be. Give them the freedom to be who they are. Let them see the world differently to you. You don't have to wear their costume. There's enough room in the universe for all the superheroes. You do you, Batman. Let Peter Parker figure out how to navigate the world with his Spidey senses.

The Problem with Superpowers

The real problem with superpowers is that at some point, they will stop working. They just will. They will be taken away from you because the universe wants to show you what you are not, so that you can uncover what you are and where your true power lies.

One of my most trusted superpowers was being the 'good girl'. The ethically superior, never-did-anything-wrong, nice-to-everyone superhero. A few years ago, when things fell apart, that perception of me changed. Overnight, I became the villain – for the first time in my life. It was shocking and humbling. I tried really hard to let go of the attachment to how I was being perceived. I grieved the loss of friendships, of my community, of those I assumed would know me better. Riddled with anxiety about what others thought, I lost chunks of my life. For the first time in 20 years, I stepped back from my acting career. I couldn't be in audition rooms where I felt everyone hated me. I stopped teaching. I withdrew from friends.

What surprised me the most, even as I was going through it all, was how deeply attached I was to being *perceived* as the good girl. I knew the truth. I knew in my heart of hearts I was sitting in my ethics and morals, and felt I had done the right thing. But it wasn't enough. I needed others to see it, too. And so, the 'good girl' had to die. She wasn't making me powerful. She was making me powerless. With my superpower gone, I was just another truly flawed human, bumbling around, trying to find my way. It wasn't easy. A part of you dies when you lose your superpower and the grief is real. I had no spark, like 22 in Disney's *Soul*. I had to start again in discovering who I was and what brought me a sense of meaning. But I was liberated. Liberated from being perfect. Liberated from holding on so tight to doing the 'right thing'. And in liberating myself, by allowing messiness and imperfection, I let others off the hook. I'm more compassionate when people make mistakes. There's more grey in my life, less black and white. Dogma is gone, replaced by openness, acceptance and humility.

Losing my superpower softened and freed me. I sincerely hope all you people-pleasing perfectionists get it knocked out of you, too. Sooner rather than later. Because when life puts you on your knees and takes away your costume, what you're left with is nothing. And that, my friends, is the beginning of everything.

Humility is your access point to who you really are and how strong you can be.

Strength in Humility and Vulnerability

'Vulnerability sounds like truth and feels like courage. Truth and courage aren't always comfortable, but they're never weakness.'
Brené Brown

Brené Brown's 20 years of research, across tens of thousands of subjects, has proven that humility and vulnerability are sure signs of strength. They are now considered key aspects of leadership, infiltrating major corporations across the board. Vulnerability opens up channels that are otherwise closed.

Back to Disney. In Disney Pixar's animated film *Inside Out*, it's the vulnerable character Sadness who connects our hero Riley to her community when she needs them most, in a way Joy and the other characters (emotions) can't.

Moments of humility are opportunities to see what you're made of. When all your defences are down and none of your tricks work, you have no other choice but to look inside.

Pema Chodron, American Tibetan Buddhist, had a quote stuck on her wall. It read: 'Only to the extent that we expose ourselves over and over to annihilation can that which is indestructible in us be found.'

You want inner strength? That's the ticket right there. It's not found in the external – in your job, body, face, brains, work ethic, charm, charisma, money, status. It's not obtained when you are the brightest, shiniest Instagram version of yourself. It's discovered internally, when everything else fades away. It's the indestructible part of you that cannot be extinguished.

It's not available in your mani-pedis, tans, waxes, laser, botox, colour and cuts, clothes, coffees, cocktails, kudos, swipeability, visibility, reachability, sexibility, flexibility, strengthability, sellability or bankability. For some of us, those things may be part of this modern thing you call life. But your invincibility lies beyond all that business.

There's nothing wrong with all that business. I quite like my business. I like my costume. I like my superpowers. I'm sure you do, too. But we have to find a way to enjoy our business and at the same time be okay when it's all taken away from us. When we're forced to check in.

Life doesn't humble us to be an asshole. It just wants us to check in, instead of out. So, we strip it back, check in and discover who we really are. Then we can put on the costume when we want and play dress-ups with the knowledge that there is no kryptonite that can take us down. No Infinity Gauntlet. No Joker. No Endgame. As David Guetta and Sia assert, you are 'titanium'.

Key Takeaways

- We misunderstand that we are just this personality self, so we spend a lot of time reinforcing that, instead of the deeper part of the self.

- We reinforce it by putting on the costume of ourselves and then believing we are that, instead of recognising that we are playing dress-ups.

- We all have a superpower that we will lose at some point, so we can experience who and what we truly are.

- True inner strength is found when we lose our superpowers. It's available in our vulnerability and humility.

REFLECTION QUESTIONS

1. When do you like to be right? Where, and with whom?

2. What feeling arises when you want to assert your rightness?

3. Think of a moment when life humbled you. What did that experience teach you?

EXERCISE
CATCHING YOUR RIGHTNESS

The first step is always noticing the 'rightness' when it arises, and catching it. This is 90 per cent of the work. This week, make it your mission to notice the moments when you want to be right. When it happens, notice the feeling associated with it and let it well up in your body. Feel the feeling, and separate it from your rightness or need to act on it. Try to take a pause – take three conscious breaths before you do anything. (This is great for family holidays when all the buttons get pushed.)

CHAPTER 7

Attachment and Aversion

'A feeling of aversion or attachment towards something is your clue that there's work to be done.'

Ram Dass

Attachment

So, you come into this world with the misunderstanding of who and what you are and where you get your strength from. You believe you are just this personality self, so you put on your costume and convince yourself and everyone else that that's who you are. You figure out what your superpowers are and, convinced they are your only source of power, use them to the best of your ability. (Until they stop working and you are forced to discover who you are beyond them.)

Then, you spend the rest of your life reinforcing the ego by moving towards people, places and things you like and away from those you have an aversion to. You bounce between these two for the rest of your days, pouring your energy into this game of like/dislike ping-pong, reinforcing the pattern each time you do. But, the more we reinforce the things we like, the more attached to them we get.

Attachment is your desire to cling to the things and people you love, as though they are a life raft and without them you may drown. But, if you understand who and what you are – if you spend some time connecting inside, not out, to that part of yourself that's beyond your costume – then you won't fear drowning. Because you won't rely on anything or anyone else to fill the void inside you. You won't be seeking a home outside of yourself in a place or person. You will be able to love freely, because you are already whole and home.

The point is not to avoid love. We should love. And love big! With every part of our being. The point is to feel what it opens up for you. How it plugs you right into a universal source – where time disappears and you're immersed in presence and union. This feeling isn't coming from something outside of you. It's already within you. It *is* you. You are love. You've just forgotten, and life is here to remind you.

So, there's no need to cling to love. There's no need to hold on tight to something you can't lose. You only grasp because you believe it can provide you with something it simply can't – feelings of worthiness, validation, permanence and certainty. It's never going to give you those. Not in the long run.

Know what love is. Know what life is. Know who you are. Trust that you have the boundless inner strength to let people be who they are and that you have the capacity to love greatly, even knowing that loss is part of the deal. Never trade your love with the expectation that anyone or anything can make you feel happy or safe. They are not your medicine. *You* are.

Attachment comes from desire. Make it a point in your life to understand the way desire operates for you specifically. Because desire undermines all of us. We are caught in a cycle of always wanting something. You want a coffee, so you get one and satiate that desire. Then you concentrate on work for a few minutes, and the craving creeps in again. You want a croissant or a chai, or to check your phone. It's like an itch you just can't scratch. Get curious about how this constant craving plays out in you. Watch your eternal hankering for one thing, then the next and the next. It's just energy moving through you in a very particular way. Observe what happens when you don't follow your desire. I'm always fascinated by what comes up for me and how challenging it is when I cut out sugar. The last time I did it, I realised how much I used sugar for pleasure and reward. I was working and parenting so hard, not socialising at all, let alone dating, and my only source of joy at home alone every night was a bowl of ice cream or chocolate. For some people, it's a few glasses of wine. The learning for me was that I really needed to find more joy and play in my life. If all my fun was coming from a packet, my life was seriously out of balance. In meditation, it's why we try not to move every time there is discomfort or an itch. The committing to stillness, to sit with whatever arises and not follow the desire to wriggle or scratch, helps to harness this ability to work with desire.

One of the ethical practices Patanjali outlines in the *Yoga Sutras* is non-grasping or greedless-ness. There's a contraction when you hold on to things so tight. It indicates that you have a lack of faith that there will always be enough for everyone, including you, and that you will be okay, come what may.

> 'Yoga is the state where you are missing nothing.'
> Shri Brahmananda Saraswati

The more you connect to the part of you beyond your personality self, the more you move to a place of wholeness. Where you're no longer hankering. No longer craving. No longer obsessing over people, work, food, clothes, shopping, money or anything outside of yourself.

In order to do that, find what connects you to the feeling that nothing is missing. When do you feel completely present, peaceful, connected and content? Like there's nowhere to go, nothing to grasp. Find that place and get more of it into your life.

Aversion

There are the people we love, and then there are the people we don't. 'Those' people ... you know the ones. I mean, it's just *so* annoying. You do all the work. You do your CrossFit, yoga, Pilates, acupuncture, kinesiology, NET (Neuro Emotional Technique) and NLP (neurolinguistic programming) therapy. You see your therapist, go on a retreat and sit in silence in the mountains for ten days. You bathe in magnesium salts, cut out coffee, break up with sugar and give up (okay, cut down on) alcohol. You swim in the ocean, do some goddess dancing and breathwork and read all the Brené Brown, Glennon Doyle and Elizabeth Gilbert you can stomach. And you feel better, you know? Calm. At peace. Zen AF. And then … *they* come along. Those people who push every button you thought you'd self-helped away.

'Those' people are your most potent teachers. They hold up a mirror and reveal your untold vulnerabilities. Pema Chodron talks about the concept of *shenpa* in Buddhism, or our inherent capacity to get triggered. Let's say you're on a date. You know that moment when you're sitting there chatting away, your date game is strong and … BOOM. You don't know what you said, but they've pulled away from you energetically. A wall has come down. Conversely, your date, who just moments ago was the star of your fantasy wedding, says something that triggers you and makes you withdraw. That's shenpa.

The problem is, as you continue to move away from everything you have an aversion to, your world shrinks and you keep reaffirming the trivial world you have curated for yourself, of which you are the centre. In doing so, you miss out on being part of the immeasurable universe. There's no room for growth or expansion. There's no strength in that. It's limited, like a horse wearing blinkers.

The more you reinforce aversion, the more you move towards a state of resentment and hatred. And that place will bleed you dry. It'll take up all your mental and energetic real estate. As the famous AA quote (credited to several different people, but consensus says it was originally Malachy McCourt) goes, 'Resentment is like drinking poison and waiting for the other person to die.' Aversion poisons you and shrinks the possibilities in your life.

The inner strength, then, is found in noticing when you're triggered and *softening,* instead of hardening. It's in seeking to understand – to ask 'why?' – and keep the door open, instead of slamming it shut. It takes courage to accept that others have different ideas and opinions from you. It takes nerve to listen openly, and agree to disagree. It is brave to sit in curiosity, instead of cutting people and things off.

This is not to say that sometimes aversion isn't showing up for good reason – when it's screaming at you to set a boundary or move away from someone because you are genuinely not safe. Don't ignore red flags. This is when discernment and intuition serve you well.

Intuition

Intuition is our higher wisdom. It's beyond the mind. It feels things at a cellular level. It can be best described as a feeling of deep knowing.

There's no doubt or confusion. You don't know why, but you feel it in your bones. That knowledge is just as valuable as the mind discerning and analysing the information and experience it's being given. Learn to connect with your intuition and trust it. The times I've felt it, and ignored it, have not been pretty. I don't learn things gracefully. You know, there are some people who get a little tap on the shoulder from the universe and they listen? Yeah, that's not me. I like to learn the hard way. Taps on the shoulder don't work. I get hit by a bus, and then I bandage myself up and try again. Until I get hit by a train. And I still don't listen. So, the universe just puts a big old bomb in my life. And then I'm like, *Ah, okay universe. Got it.* Don't be like me. Be graceful in your learning. If there's a little red flag and your intuition spots it, listen. Don't wait for a bomb to wake you up.

Working with Aversion

I get very interested when I have an aversion to someone or something because, when it arises, I know there's some juicy self-knowledge that is about to surface. It often appears in judging others, in thinking I'm better than them in some way or that I am somehow so very different. It rears its ugly head on social media when I see someone with vastly different politics and opinions from me. I want to stay awake for it all, because, let's face it – you can't make good decisions on the battlefield of life when you are triggered AF.

You only make intelligent, fearless decisions from a place of strength when you are connected to the part of you that understands who you are. The part of you that no longer believes you are just the Batman costume. The part of you that loves your life, getting a chai, mani-pedi and date night with your beloved. And, at the same time, when the rug is pulled out from under you – you're in lockdown and can't access your favourite things or you lose someone or something you love – you feel it all, but it doesn't destroy you. When someone triggers you and you want to pull away, get curious about what the aversion is all about instead of closing down. What sits under you, wanting to pull away from someone or something? Why do you feel the need to get distance from them? Can you use them as a vehicle for growth and self-knowledge?

The self-knowledge you obtain through love and hate serves as a gateway to soften the tendency to create division. It shows you where you are stuck and where there is still work to do in order for you to connect more and separate less.

The connectivity to your costume-less deeper self is the true life raft that will save you from drowning. All you have to do is stop the game of craving-and-aversion ping-pong. Stop waiting for others to light you up and, instead, become a firefly.

Key Takeaways

- We have a tendency to move towards people, places and things we like, and away from those we have an aversion to.
- Attachment is when you feel you may drown without the life raft of people and things you love.
- When you feel whole, you don't expect others to fill you up.
- There's nothing wrong with love, but remember that it doesn't come from outside of you. It's in you – you are love.
- People who trigger you are your most potent teachers.
- Aversion becomes resentment and hatred, which will bleed you dry.
- Instead of hardening when triggered, learn to soften.

REFLECTION QUESTIONS

1. What, or whom, are you strongly attached to in your life? What aspects of that attachment bring pleasure and what aspects bring pain?

2. Spend the week noticing when you have an aversion to someone, something or somewhere. Get curious about where it's coming from and why it wants to create distance or separation.

EXERCISE
LOVING-KINDNESS MEDITATION

Studies have shown that loving-kindness meditation has many benefits, including increasing vagal tone, which boosts positive emotions and feelings of social connection, increases compassion and empathy, and decreases bias towards one another, which are all qualities that help even out the cycle of craving and aversion.

Choose a comfortable seat or lie down on your back. Take a moment to bring your awareness into your physical body, noticing the quality of your body, the quality of your mind and the quality of your breath. Shift your attention back to your physical body and into the space around your heart. How does the heart space feel? Notice any sensations. Notice your breath. Don't modify the breath in any way. Allow it to be natural, moving of its own accord.

Start by wishing yourself to be happy and free from suffering, and send yourself love. Next, think of someone you love, someone close to you that comes easily to mind. Picture them happy. Send them loving kindness, and wish them to be free from suffering. Start with those close to you. And then as you move to the next person, and the next, let the circle widen.

Don't be surprised if people arise that you don't expect. See them as happy and free, send them loving kindness, and move on. When you've finished, notice your breath. Shift all of your awareness back into the heart space. How does it feel? Take a deep, slow inhale and a deep, slow exhale to let the breath go.

CHAPTER 8

Fireflies

'To be Jedi is to face the truth, and choose. Give off
light, or darkness, Padawan. Be a candle, or the night.'

Yoda

Produce Your Own Light

I love fireflies. These incredible glow-worms with wings are bioluminescent creatures, which means they produce their own light. Glow-worms shouldn't fly – they're worms – but these ones do. Fireflies just grow wings. Their light doesn't require a battery or cord; they have their own energy source. They don't try to steal other fireflies' light. They don't dim their own light to make other fireflies feel better. They don't feel 'less than' when other fireflies are twinkling around in their luminous splendour. In fact, fireflies are known to flash in bright synchronicity with one another, just because. And how's this – the chemical reaction that occurs in the little firefly makes it the most efficient light in the world. It is so powerful that the chemical it uses, luciferin, is now harvested (unfortunately one of the reasons the population of fireflies is in steady decline) and used in all sorts of scientific pursuits.

Now, I don't want your light to be harvested, but I do hope you create your own vivid luminescence. Don't rely on an external source. Don't depend on others to light you up. Find your own sweet luciferin.

There are many ways to do this. Some of us find it naturally through activities such as running or surfing, when all the other noise disappears and we are wholly present. Anything that connects you to your soul, your spark, and draws you in will foster your relationship with your inner firefly. For some, it's creative pursuits such as painting or music. For others, it's cooking, swimming or meditating.

Once you find it, don't let anyone take it away from you. According to yoga mythology, Garuda, an eagle-like sun bird, emerged from his egg shining as bright as the sun (or as a diamond, Ri-Ri style). He was so luminous that the gods got jealous and begged him to dim his light. Don't dim your light for anyone. Ever. It's your light to shine. It's your life to live. It always has been. Be like Dorothy and her red slippers. Because home is inside you – it always was. As the good witch Glinda says: 'You've always had the power, my dear.'

When You Meet Your Soul

Unless you've been living under a rock, you will have heard of the greatest heroine of our modern time: Elsa. If you don't know who I'm talking about, you definitely don't have kids and you need to stop reading and go and watch the Disney phenomenon that is *Frozen* and *Frozen 2*. (Spoiler alert: if you haven't seen them, I'm about to ruin them for you, so be warned.)

In the first film, we see our heroine – like all good heroines – on a journey, becoming victorious in a crisis and returning home transformed.

Throughout *Frozen*, we witness Elsa trying to wrangle her superpowers, which happen to be turning things into ice (as the title suggests). One of her big lessons (and, therefore, 'the' song) in the first film is about surrender and letting go. She yields to the chaos of not being able to control her powers and takes herself far away to where she can't accidentally freeze anyone (like her sister, Anna – which, of course, she inadvertently does – but, don't worry, Anna gets unfrozen). Another lesson is that great love can conquer all. Because, as we know, it always comes back to love.

In *Frozen 2*, however (which I believe is a far superior film, but we can argue about that another time), she is on a slightly different journey. This is her journey of self-discovery. The journey you need to embark on, too, if you wish to connect with your inner power. In the sequel, we find Elsa restless because she can hear a voice (singing, of course – it's Disney). She's not sure where it's coming from or what it is, but she knows that she must follow it wherever it takes her.

So, off she goes, leaving her long-suffering sister behind once more, because like all journeys of the soul, some things you have to do alone. She relinquishes everything and everyone she knows and loves. She makes great sacrifices and takes unimaginable risks. She crosses dangerous territory and stormy seas. One of her greatest lessons here is having courage to go into the unknown (cue song), and part of what holds her through that is faith. It's only by going into the unknown that she can find the voice which is ... drumroll please ... her. The voice is her. She meets her self, her spirit, her soul. When she meets her spirit (dramatic music kicks in), finally she receives her full power and can control it (therefore, she gets a new frock – because, Disney). She becomes way more powerful than she ever imagined. And, this time, Elsa doesn't return home, because she is already there.

This is what happens when we meet our true nature, our spirit, our soul. Most of us are disconnected from it, so we have to go on a big journey of self-discovery, sacrifice and faith in order to reconnect to it. But hopefully we do so without freezing the city (or our loved ones) in the process.

It's an Inside Job

If you desire to connect to your inner strength – to step into the full capacity of your soul, to meet your spirit and light yourself up – you're going to have to turn your attention inside. You will have to spend some time in stillness, pull your awareness internally and sit with yourself. It's just not possible to tap into your limitless power without doing so.

Just like in the *Gita*, Arjuna's arrow has to be pulled in before it's propelled out towards his purpose. The arrow of intention is useless without the drawing into the bow, as it can't be projected – there's no movement without the retraction and pause.

Being still, and pulling in, can feel like contraction. But this is the eternal dance of the universe. Things move between contraction and expansion, over and over. It's why your breath has so much to teach you. During every inhale, you're expanding. During every exhale, there's contraction. We need both. One can't exist without the other.

The times when we are contracted in stillness and quiet are just as fruitful as the times of expansion where we're moving out into the world with our creativity and actions. They are necessary for growth. How often do you 'Nemo' your life away, knowing you're run-down or you should stop and regroup but, instead, you just keep swimming ... only to end up crashing and burning in some way. If you're always in activity and you don't find stillness, life will still you. And it's often not pretty when it does.

I remember thinking that after Australia had the 2019–2020 summer of bushfires, followed by the 2020–2021 lockdowns, that the universe was sending us all to our rooms to have a good, long, hard think about how we'd been behaving. For the first time in our lives, we were all given permission slips to stay home from school. Even in the pervading sense of uncertainty and despair, there was a collective feeling of relief in just not 'doing' for a moment. Instead, we could 'be' human 'beings'. All the parents I know talked about how much easier life was without all the kids' parties, sports and activities. Many friends made radical life changes, as the pause allowed them to reflect on the way they had been living, and they didn't like what they saw. They wanted a life of purpose and meaning. To have time to bake bread, surf at lunchtime and walk in the park. They wanted to live their life on Earth. Sometimes, it takes stopping your life to learn to live it again.

Going It Alone

In his 1988 bestselling book, *Solitude: A Return to the Self,* leading psychiatrist and physician Anthony Storr challenged the existing status quo that the psychology world had held until then – that interpersonal relationships were the main source of happiness for individuals. Storr's book argued that solitude was just as important for an individual's wellbeing. Citing a vast number of extraordinary scholars and artists, from Beethoven to Beatrix Potter, he argued that solitude was essential for creativity, productivity, progress and happiness. Solitude, he suggested, was good for us.

I think it's really important here to make the distinction between 'solitude' and 'loneliness'. Solitude can be defined as the state of being alone. Loneliness, on the other hand, is a feeling of sadness about being socially isolated. Loneliness can be normal, it can show us when it's time to reconnect with others, but it can also be an indicator of underlying disease when those feelings become overwhelming. That's when we need to call in extra support. And if we see others feeling lonely, we do something about it. We check in. We connect. We take care of each other.

There is a case that if we all practised solitude regularly, we would not experience loneliness. Because solitude allows us to connect with parts of ourselves not dictated by external things. And it's the external things that often get us into all sorts of trouble. When we are seeking happiness and fulfilment outside of ourselves, we are inevitably going to suffer.

Because, on the one hand, yes, you are part of – as Madonna reminds us – the material world. But, on the other hand, nothing comes from outside of you. The external just helps you experience the internal. You have to understand how your mind works in the material world. How it is always seeking pleasure, and avoiding pain, through external objects. But the reality is, it all comes from you. All of the things you *feel* when you move towards people and experiences – all the inner strength you foster from connecting to others – it's inside, not out. Focus inwards and sense that. That inner strength is who you are.

At some point, no matter how much love and support you have behind you, you're going to have to go it alone. Even if you have an army, like Arjuna, there will come a time when you'll have to stand on the battlefield, connect to your inner strength and face the music, solo. There are certain things in life only you can do. But when you've spent some time in solitude and forged an unbreakable bond with your soul, you will, as Yoda suggests, feel the force. And this, my friend, is how you Luke Skywalker any battle that comes your way.

Key Takeaways

- Find your own inner light source, like a firefly.
- When you connect to your soul, you'll step into your power source.
- In life, sometimes you're in contraction and sometimes you're in expansion.
- In contraction and stillness, pulling in, we connect to our strength.
- Look inside, not out – that's where you connect to your inner strength.
- At some point, you'll have to go it alone on the battlefield, feel the force within and Luke Skywalker that battle.

REFLECTION QUESTIONS

1. How do you feel when other people shine bright like a firefly? What sits under this feeling? Let this self-knowledge shine a light on what work you need to do.

2. How do you relate to times of contraction versus expansion? Is there one you find easier?

3. What is your relationship with solitude?

EXERCISE
THREE-PART BREATH
(DIRGA PRANAYAMA)

In this practice, we experience who and what we are through the breath.

Lie on your back comfortably. Take a moment to notice where you most feel breath moving into the body. Maybe it's in the chest, or quite high near the collarbones. Place your hands on your lower belly. As you inhale, take a slow, deep breath and consciously direct it into the lower belly. As you exhale, let the breath go – don't control the exhale. Do that a few times, slowly stretching out the inhale, but then letting the breath out naturally on the exhale. Shift your hands and awareness to your ribs. As you inhale, send breath to the side and back ribs. As you exhale, let the breath go. Take a few rounds. Then shift your awareness to the chest and place your hands under your collarbones, this time sending breath into the chest for a few rounds. Place the hands back on the belly and leave them there as you inhale into belly, then the ribs, then the chest, filling the body with breath. At the top of the inhale, let the breath go. Take a few rounds of this full-body breath. When you are ready, breathe as normal and reflect on how you feel now.

CHAPTER 9

Surfing

'You are the sky. Everything else – it's just the weather.'

Pema Chodron

Recently, Gabriel joined Surf Academy (run by real-life superhero Bondi lifeguard Dean Gladstone), a program for kids aimed at building confidence in the ocean. As a Sydney kid growing up on the beaches, he needs to know how to survive in the surf.

Unfortunately, just as the program began, the surfing conditions turned apocalyptic thanks to an epic bluebottle season and cyclonic winds up north. Not one to take risks, I watched G and his reluctant mates paddle off into the depths of a very choppy North Bondi, further than I've ever been brave enough to swim. A couple of them were stung by bluebottles and all were pummelled by rough waves more than once, so there were tears and tirades aplenty. When the lesson ended, G stormed up the beach like a little seal in his wetsuit, furiously pulled off his goggles, threw them in the sand and screamed, 'They tried to murder me!' and started a monologue about how it was the worst day of his life.

Two days later, we were back at the beach and he was playing and bodysurfing the waves with a confidence I'd never seen in him before.

This is what the mind does: jumps from thought to thought, putting everything you experience through the wave-crashing filter of your own perception.

The Monkey Mind

According to Buddhist principles, the 'monkey mind' describes the tendency of the mind to move around with the characteristics of a monkey – the constant chatter, jumping and swinging from branch to branch, thought to thought. In the *Yoga Sutras*, Patanjali describes this same tendency of the mind to turn constantly. A whirling mind cannot be present, because it's distracted by thoughts. The yogic practices are designed to interrupt the unconscious turning of the mind in the same way Buddhist and mindfulness practices are designed to transcend the monkey mind. In this way, you come into the present moment and connect with that deeper part of the self.

The distracted mind comes from the ego via our thoughts. That is, the part of you that is constantly putting everything you experience through the filter of your perception. There's nothing wrong with this. It's called being human. As Tibetan Buddhist Yongey Mingyur Rinpoche says, 'The monkey mind is neither bad nor good.' There's no point making it your enemy. You need to make friends with it. When you sit down to meditate, for example, you start to notice your thoughts jumping around. If you can witness those thoughts, like waves, then you can't be those thoughts. You must be separate from them in order to be able to see them. You witness the mind turning, and then get familiar with it. Over time, the more we notice the distracted mind, the less power it has over us.

Your mind is like the ocean – it's vast, deep and still. But, on the surface, there are thoughts, like waves, moved around by external factors such as the weather, which the ocean can't control. This is how we start to unite with our limitless potential. The weather, the external world, will continue to turn and provide distraction. And although the waves and the ocean cannot be separated, it's your job to remember that you are the ocean, not just the waves. You witness the waves, you watch the monkey mind, and at the same time you experience that there is this part of you not subject to change.

All the best sea creatures lie in the deepest, darkest depths. Like the miraculous bioluminescent creatures that create their own light (like fireflies!). But most of us are too afraid of the dark to dive that deep, so we swim on the surface, where our thoughts move around like waves. Just like the ocean, sometimes the surf is big and a shitshow of chaos. Other days, it's small and manageable. We spend most of our lives thinking we are the waves; we are our thoughts, and we get caught up in them. Sometimes, we surf with joy and ease, even a little fear can be exhilarating. But, other times, we get dumped and pulled under and drown in the madness of the mind and, it feels like, as G so aptly said, it may kill us.

It's your job to get a bit of separation from your thoughts through mindfulness practices, so you become familiar with the crazy patterns of the mind and recognise that you are not the waves. You are not your thoughts. If you can see them, if you can observe them, then you cannot also be them.

You are the ocean. Vast and deep and connected to everyone and everything else in the universe you inhabit. The more you connect to that part of yourself – the expansive oceanic mind, the part that is not subject to change – the more you understand who and what you truly are. Beyond the breakers. Because the tide will ebb and flow. But the sea, you see, is always there. When we spend more time connecting to that part of ourselves, then, and only then, will we be able to ride the waves, no matter the weather. We will dive deep and swim far. We may still get dumped and pummelled. We may even get carried away by the undercurrent. But we will never, ever, feel lost at sea. Because we cannot be lost when we are home.

Key Takeaways

- The mind has a tendency to jump around.
- Use the present moment to anchor the mind and become familiar with its movements and patterns.
- Start to feel that you are not just the waves (thoughts) but also the ocean (that deeper part of you not subject to change).

REFLECTION QUESTIONS

1. When do you find it hard to stay in the present moment?

2. What kinds of thoughts feel like big waves and currents?

3. What thoughts do you notice go in a loop? The ones that come again and again? I like to interrupt them with a conscious breath or by shifting my attention to something such as a count or mantra.

EXERCISE
NADA YOGA

Nada yoga helps us pull in, so we can connect with that deep, internal part of the self. When we practise nada yoga, we notice how quickly we hear sounds, give them a label and make meaning of the external world. So, as we learn deeper listening, we try to hear things for what they are – vibration – and then eventually hear the internal sounds, which allows us to connect with who we are. It's like diving down into the oceanic depths of the soul. But first, we just learn to listen.

Choose a comfortable seat. Take a moment to notice how your body, mind and breath feel. Shift your attention to listening. Notice sounds around you. Hear the most distant sounds. Be aware of how quickly we shift into giving a label to what we hear. A bird sings and we immediately categorise it: 'There's a bird.' Instead, try to just hear a sound for what it is – vibration – and then move on to the next sound. Over time, listen to sounds closer and closer, until you hear the soft sound of your breath. Turn your listening inwards. Can you hear your heart beating, your blood flowing? What else is there? Sit and listen to your internal landscape, to the more subtle and deep parts of the ocean self.

CHAPTER 10

Discipline and Sacrifice

'Self-discipline burns away impurities
and kindles the sparks of divinity.'

Yoga Sutra 2:43 (translated by B.K.S. Iyengar)

Tapas

Who doesn't love tapas? Oh, the many hours I spent inhaling wine and grazing tapas behind Toledo's infamous doors and Barcelona's iconic tiled walls. The teeny-tiny bars across Spain hold some of my most joyous memories. Those little bite-sized delights bring so much joy, don't they? I would eat tapas every meal if I could. You get lots of variety, it's always full of flavour and satisfies the senses ... for a moment. Because those little plates are oh-so small, you never really feel full in the same way you do after a 'proper' meal.

'*Tapas*' from the yogic perspective means discipline and sacrifice. And it also brings us great joy. Only, it's not the snack-sized fleeting variety. It fosters the kind of strength that, once experienced, lasts a lifetime and beyond. It tastes better than anything you can imagine and makes you feel truly full, and whole, again.

Don't get me wrong. As we spoke about earlier, those bite-sized fleeting moments are full of meaning. They have much to teach us. But many of us spend our lives trying to make those magic moments on weekends and holidays, with our morning coffee and snack. But there comes a point in your life where, no matter how much you travel or how many extraordinary tiny experiences you have, inevitably they end. Because that's the deal in the manifest world. Things begin, they have a middle and they end. (Unless you're Edward from *Twilight*). And when it does end, so does the joy. What you are left with is yourself.

> 'Wherever you go, there you are.'
> Jon Kabat-Zinn

If you are expending all your energy chasing sensory experiences that are transient, you are foregoing something way better. You are passing up the opportunity to experience who you really are, which is not transitory. And you need your precious energy to be invested in the pursuit of that, which is where *tapas* comes in.

If you desire more strength, there's going to be some heat. Self-discipline will become a key aspect of your life. It's the tapas that insists you turn off Netflix's latest series – no, not 'just one more episode' – so you can get enough sleep, get up to meditate and make a healthy breakfast before the kids, work, the dog and all the rest. Its passion talks louder than all your excuses. It drags your sorry ass to the yoga studio or gym on a rainy, cold day. It tells you not to shove that packet of Oreos in your mouth, or social media in your mind, as you eat and scroll your feelings away at 11.19pm. It invites you to purify the body and mind from the inside out, becoming disciplined in what you put in it and how you treat it. It makes you pause before you send that angry email in response to your narcissistic colleague. It stops you from saying what you can't take back in an argument. It tells you not to speak but instead listen when your emotions are high. It's fundamental in managing how well you take care of yourself and how you expend your energy.

A lack of discipline is considered one of the main obstacles to yoga, or to feeling whole. This is why we need it so badly. It's like any other relationship – the road to inner strength is challenging and lonely, and boredom will arise. Ask anyone who has survived long-term marriages and intimate relationships. Your relationship with self is the longest one you'll have – it's a lifer! But we also know that when you work through that boredom and face obstacles with love, humility, faith, passion and discipline, a deeper, unshakeable connectivity with yourself, and others, arises.

As you control how you relate to your body, breath and mind, you become an observer of yourself. You perceive your shadows, your darkness, your resistance, and work with them. You connect with something more profound than your everyday mundane self. In self-discipline, you break habit patterns and transform at a cellular level. You look around and see your life changing in subtle and epic ways, which helps to galvanise your passion to keep going.

In this way, tapas nurtures faith. The more we feel the results of self-discipline, the more we want to do it. It doesn't feel so much like work because we know how good it tastes. Once you taste a freshly baked chocolate cake you just made, you never resent making a cake again.

I'm not a baker. (That's an understatement.) Cooking is not my thing. But for Gabriel's fifth birthday, I decided to make his cake. I didn't have any baker's equipment. I took myself to Target for a $7 cake tin and those turning-blender thingies. I asked a friend for her most foolproof recipe. I bought all the ingredients, including mint Mentos, as per G's topping request. Friends championed me, but also doubted me (like Arjuna with his doubts in the *Gita*). Oh, ye of little faith! It was hard work for a novice – doing all the steps, getting the timing right – and, in the end, it was no masterpiece. I may have overfilled the $7 cake tin and made way too much icing. It may have been lopsided. I may have missed the memo about waiting until the icing cools down, so there was a Mentos icing-slide. But my goodness, it tasted good. And the joy and satisfaction it brought to both myself and G (who proudly declared to anyone who would listen that his mum had baked it) was worth every precious second.

Sacrifice

Here's the universal deal: if you want something, you have to give something up. You want to climb the corporate ladder, you'll probably have to give up some time with family and friends. You want to get fit and healthy, you'll probably have to give up your morning sleep-ins to exercise and swap your Mentos cake for a protein shake.

They say we can have it all, and I believe we can. Just not all at once. In the early days of parenting, you have to give up lots of things you used to put your time and energy into because it's all directed at the small ones. Especially if you're juggling work, too. Socialising, exercise and 'me' time will take a back seat. But nothing can replace the love you feel for those little maniacs, and it tastes better than anything else. On the other hand, if you're single and ready to mingle, if you really want a relationship, you'll have to make sacrifices in order for it to work. You'll have to put time and energy into the dating game, which we all know is no joke. Then, you have to do the dance of getting to know someone you like, which reminds you how exhausting relationships are and why you avoided them in the first place. And then, you have to learn to compromise in order to sustain the complexities of a long-lasting union.

This is tapas. In every moment of every day, you make choices. You can't have it all at once, so what's it going to be? It's up to you to figure out what you believe in and what is important to you, and then take actions that support that. If Saturday morning is your time to go for your weekly run but is also your only window to bake a lopsided Mentos cake for your kid, then you have to figure out what you're going to sacrifice. Often, you have to give up something you are comfortable with in order to receive something bigger and better. Usually, the greater the reward, the larger the sacrifice.

So, start with the tiny. Practise giving something up, something you desire, every day. To make it even more potent, give it to someone else. As Shri Pattabhi Jois famously said: 'Practice and all is coming.' All! Maybe even a warm, lopsided, love-infused Mentos cake.

Key Takeaways

- If you want access to your inner strength, there's going to be some heat. It will require some discipline.
- If you want to get something, you have to give something up. That's the universal deal.
- Every day we make choices. You can't have everything at once, so what's it going to be?

REFLECTION QUESTIONS

1. Think of a time when you had to make a sacrifice. What did you give up and what did you receive?

2. Is there something you really want, but know it requires sacrifice or discipline you haven't yet engaged in?

3. If you could have anything you wanted, what would you be willing to give up?

4. What area of your life requires more discipline? What steps can you take to start the process?

EXERCISE
DELAY GRATIFICATION

Spend the week delaying gratification. If you have chocolate every night (hypothetically, of course, not that I do …), see if you can wait until Friday. Notice how your cravings arise every day and see if you can put them off. Reflect on how it feels to do this.

CHAPTER 11

Faith

'Faith gives us strength and allows us to remain
increasingly unshaken in the ups and downs of
life. We begin to receive nourishment from within.
We discover the inner source of the nectar of
contentment and joy. It brings us fulfilment and the
power, stamina and agility necessary to pursue our path.'

Ram Dass

The *Gita* said it, Patanjali said it, George Michael said it – you gotta have faith. If you want to weather the great storms of life, you'll need to get intimate with faith, or *shraddha* in Sanskrit. Faith is the *key* to your inner strength because it will hold you steady in a way nothing else can. It's connected to that firefly light inside you.

When you hear the F-word, some of you will have a visceral reaction. It can create aversion and mistrust because our cultural understanding of faith is wrapped up in dogma. But I'm not talking about blind following. I'm talking about the profound sense of trust that everything is exactly as it should be – that the universe has your back, always. But not in the sense that the universe has your back so it gives you everything you want. Rather, the innate belief that the universe has your back because it's providing opportunities for you to grow. It's giving you medicine to evolve and become the strong, resilient warrior that you are. Medicine doesn't always taste good, but it can be necessary and powerful when we need it most. As the saying goes, no mud, no lotus.

When you live your life in this way, understanding that the universe is conspiring for your growth, everything becomes more easeful. You perceive challenges as potential for growth. It changes the frequency you face obstacles with and gives you the stamina to 'just keep swimming', like Nemo. Because come what may, whatever the outcome, you know there will be some juicy learning along the way.

Trusting in the Unknown

Elsa's first big song in *Frozen 2* is 'Into the Unknown'. It's where she has to go in order to understand who she is. She sings about what she can feel in her bones, what she can sense but not yet see. Trusting in what you cannot yet see, trusting in the unknown, is how we foster faith.

We live in a world where seeing is believing. We rely on our senses every moment of every day to determine an experience. If I can see, feel, touch, hear, smell and taste it, then it must be true. We like to 'know', us humans. Knowing makes us feel safe in the world. It's why we wonder what's happening on our phones when they are upside down on the table as we have coffee with our friends. The problem is, the need to know gets in the way of us being completely present. All our energy (*prana*) is directed at wanting to grasp on to some solid ground, so the limitless possibilities of the currently unknown are inaccessible. The things our senses haven't even perceived yet don't get a chance to come to realisation because we close a door on them in the absence of proof.

If you want to access infallible steadiness and strength, you have to be okay with not knowing. Not knowing who has texted you in the last hour, not knowing if you're right or wrong, not knowing the outcome.

How Our Faith Gives Strength to Others

In the last few days of my grandpa's life, I lay awake at night thinking about him being in that hospital bed, having to go through this final transition of life alone. He had deeper faith than anyone I've ever known. He was a practising Catholic, went to church every day and believed that he was going home once he left his body. That knowledge gave me peace. His faith held me and provided immense strength throughout those final days. What a gift that your faith can potentially ease the suffering of those around you.

Faith and I have a complicated relationship. I've always found it very challenging, so I play with it – in the tiny, every day – to flex that muscle. Say, for example, getting a parking ticket. Through gritted teeth, I'll say, 'Thank you universe for showing me I'm so busy and distracted at the moment, that I'm running late and park last-minute somewhere I know I'll get booked.' If there's something I'm going through that feels the opposite to the universe having my back, I try to say, 'I don't understand what this is about, but I trust that there's some learning for me from this experience.'

I don't believe everything happens for a reason. That doesn't make sense to me when you witness so much suffering and violence in the world. But I do believe you can do everything in your power to build faith in your own life, so you can access greater trust and steadiness and be of service to those around you. So you can see difficult experiences as medicine for your own evolution. Sometimes the medicine is not going to taste good. We are all going to suffer, yes, but in order to rise like the phoenix again and again, we have to step out of victim mode and into a growth mindset. That's the deal with being a phoenix. If you want more light in your life, you have to play with the sun, so there's going to be some heat. You're going to get burnt. That's why there is nothing passive about waking up and taking responsibility for everything that happens in your life. It requires a great deal of courage, discipline and tenacity. It's why the *Gita* is set on a battlefield. You are not alone in your suffering. Know that. None of us is immune to pain. But if you want to rise out of the ashes, phoenix and Daenerys-Targaryen-from-*Game-of-Thrones* style, you've got to have faith in the fire that burns you.

Jealousy

Ah, the green-eyed monster. It's a very useful feeling, as it often shows you where you are stuck. Maybe it's giving you a kick in the ass to do all the things you are destined to do but have been putting off. Sometimes it signals that you are on the wrong track and steers you back towards where you were always meant to be headed. Or perhaps you need to learn more about widening your circle of compassion. It's often an indication of self-worth and faith. It signals the fear that there is just not enough for all of us and if someone else gets it, you won't. When you work on your relationship with faith, you trust there will always be enough. What is not for you will be taken away. And what is for you will never pass you by.

Taking a Leap of Faith

The story of Hanuman, the great monkey god of the Ramayana, teaches that the 'monkey mind' – which we spoke about earlier – can be disciplined, that devotion and love can be incredibly powerful, and that there is immense value in taking a leap of faith.

Before Hanuman learned to wrangle his monkey mind, he was pretty cheeky. In one of my favourite stories of his, he got greedy and ate the sun, thinking it was the biggest piece of fruit ever. Ouch.

As he became more disciplined, his strength grew, as did his love for his BFF, Rama. His devotion to Rama was illustrated as he leapt continents to save Sita, the woman Rama loved. He was tireless in his efforts, so much so that he burnt his tail in the process. The Hanuman story asks you to consider who you love, how you honour them and what you would do for them. And once you've figured that out, it says, find your strength by taking a great leap of faith. Even if it means burning your booty (or tail) along the way.

Key Takeaways

- Faith is the feeling that the universe is conspiring for your growth.
- You have to learn to be okay with not knowing.
- Our faith can support others.
- What is not for you will pass you by; what is for you will never pass you by.
- When we know what we love, sometimes we have to take a leap of faith.

REFLECTION QUESTIONS

1. How do you relate to the idea of faith?

2. Do you believe the universe has your back?

3. How would it feel if you 100 per cent believed in this? What would you do differently?

EXERCISE
FAKING FAITH

Spend the week focusing on your relationship with faith. Act as though everything that happens is the universe conspiring for your greater good, your growth. Reflect on what self-knowledge this reveals.

CHAPTER 12

So What? Now What?

'Atha yoganusasanam' ('Now, this is yoga as
I have perceived it in the natural world')
Yoga Sutra 1:1 (translation by Sharon Gannon)

Of all the words to start his life-changing book about yoga, about how to find more inner peace and strength, Patanjali chose the word *atha* or 'now'. If you understand this first word, you don't have to read the rest of the book. You're enlightened; you can go home (your real home).

Everything you need is in this very moment. When you don't hanker to be somewhere else with someone else ... eating, drinking, doing, thinking or feeling something else. Most of us can be in the present when things are pleasant. But when things aren't so great, when you're on the battlefield about to fight, not so much.

My atha, my 'now', has been extreme-sports challenging of late. I sold an apartment, bought a new one and moved house all within a month. I sold the only home G knew. They say it's one of the most stressful things you do, moving house. I did this while I had no credit card (it got skimmed), no partner to help (or yell at), an unmanageable workload, all the emotions about leaving the only nest G has known and no patience left.

In the midst of the chaos, we were racing out the door, bundling everything into the car on the way to school (late, of course), when I realised G had left his breakfast bag inside. He remembered his school bag (which is a feat most days), but not his brekkie. Apparently, I hadn't made it clear enough by leaving it next to his school bag. So, I lost my shit and screamed, 'I CAN'T DO EVERYTHING!' I told him that from now on, he will have a *timetable* in his room and a *list* of things that need to be done every day. He said quietly, 'Okay.' And then he asked if I could write them in the order that I wanted them done in.

Right there, in the heat of the atha, is the opportunity to take conscious action or to react. To blame and shame my eight-year-old for my lack of sleep and overworked stretching-myself-to-my-limit-ness, or to make a mistake, own it – acknowledge my own darkness, exhaustion and fallibility – and say I'm sorry.

I said I was sorry. And then, most importantly, I forgave myself. Life doesn't require your perfection on the battlefield. It just needs your presence, so you can wake up again and again. I went back and got the brekkie. G smiled and said he's going to use the 'stress of moving' as an excuse to lose his shit when he's a grown-up, too, one day. All was well again in the world.

Anxiety is when we are moving into the future, depression is when we are stuck in the past and peace is available only in the present moment – no matter how comfortable or uncomfortable it is. So, if nothing else, become a warrior of choosing to be in the present. The good, bad and ugly of it. The fatigue, the tears, the morning coffee, the racing for the train, the 2am feeds, the break-ups, the make-ups, the tricky marriage, the big love, the difficult conversations, the laughter-filled brunch ... your only job is to be in it. Every glorious breath. After all, we never know when we may take our last one.

Acceptance

Often, when we find ourselves on the battlefield, we get stuck in the 'buts': 'But it's not my fault' ... 'But it's not fair' ... 'But it's not right' ... 'But it's not what I wanted' ... 'But it's not what I planned' ... It might not be, but it's your responsibility to get off your butt, get over the buts and take action from where you're at now. What's done is done. So, now what?

Acceptance isn't passive. It's not apathy. It's not tough love. It's not waving a white flag in surrender. It's not laying down your weapons and walking away. It's seeing clearly, accepting what is and taking conscious action. You row away from the rocks because you see a giant cliff face. You don't give up and you don't give in – you give everything you've got to face whatever is in front of you.

When Gabriel was four, we had our first big Halloween experience. Until this point, his diet was predominantly sugar-free. I spent hours preparing nourishing, organic meals and snacks. Treats were a rare occurrence (unless he was at the grandparents', in which case all bets were off). It was our first foray into trick-or-treating and if we were going to do it, in true Coopes style, we'd go hard or go home. I mean, for kids, it's kind of like Vegas, right? All the terrible things: being allowed to dress up as something creepy or inappropriate, walk the streets on a school night with all your mates and accept buckets of candy from strangers. I mean, it doesn't get much better.

We had chosen a street in Sydney's beach-side suburb Bronte, infamous for its Halloween madness. If you buy into it, you sign up for a proper commitment to Halloween each year. Thousands of families were swarming and every house went above and beyond in decorations and confectionery output. I cringingly watched mini Dracula G, his eyes wild as he shoved handfuls of loot into his mouth, scampering from house to house as he looked over his shoulder in fear that I'd stop him at some point. As we finished, everyone descended to the playground at the end of the street. It was mayhem – like a scene from *Poltergeist* – with tonnes of candy-crack-fuelled kids screaming, trying to run the drugs out of their bodies. I watched G running around in circles until he suddenly stopped with a panicked look on his face, whipped down his pants and proceeded to do a giant sugar-OD poo on the grass in the middle of the park.

That, my friends, is a lesson in acceptance. Because what the actual f&*^ do you do in a moment like that when all eyes are on you and your shitting kid? So, here's what I did: I got a plastic bag and some wipes from some very accommodating parents and laughed until I almost peed my pants with the two friends I was there with as I picked up the poo in a doggy bag and sorted G out.

Don't desire for things to be other than they are. Don't try to control what is out of your control. It will only cause you pain. Pick up a plastic bag, grab some wipes, have a laugh and connect with others and the experience. Because there's nothing like an emergency Halloween poo in a park to humble you and remind you that sometimes you have to let go.

Surrender

Surrender doesn't mean giving up. It means doing all the work. It means learning to manage your energy, control the senses, become more mindful, get clear on your purpose, make sacrifices and have discipline and faith so that, ultimately, you can let go. As my grandpa used to say, 'Let go and let God.' Do the work and then have faith.

You've done all you can. You've played your part. Sometimes, the strength is surrendering to the results.

Non-Attachment to Results

It takes a lot to grow plants. I know this because I am not a plant whisperer. Some may consider me the opposite and the trail of dead plant destruction I've left behind me may concur. It's not my fault. It takes so many things for a plant to thrive. Take an apple tree, for example. So much has to conspire for it to bear fruit. First, the soil has to be rich and fertile. Then, the little seed – which is really just a possibility – needs to be planted in the right place as it requires nourishment from the sun and the rain. Hopefully, a tiny seedling eventually breaks through the earth and sprouts. But there are many elements that are out of the tree's control. (If you're a house plant, for example, your owner may water you too much! Or too little. Or they may put you in too much sun. Or not enough. And you have to sit there and just trust that she knows what she's doing. Hypothetically, that is.) Back to the apple tree ... Hopefully, with a lot of time, good weather and no cheeky insects or animals devouring it, branches and leaves may finally bear fruit in the form of apples. But, how's this – the apples are not for the tree. It's the job of the tree to do all the work and grow them but, ultimately, the tree must let them go.

In the same way, you have to learn not to attach to results. Do the work and then surrender to the outcome. When you are focused on results, you can't be completely in the process of whatever you are creating. Picasso didn't set out to become an award-winning painter. Albert Einstein didn't aim to be the most acclaimed scientist of all time. Had they both been attaching to results, instead of immersing themselves in creativity and curiosity, I wonder if they would have achieved all they did.

We all have a little Picasso and Einstein inside of us. We may not paint or discover the general theory of relativity, but we all have the capacity to connect to our immeasurably powerful inner strength and potential. Be in the task at hand completely, and do your best. The power of non-attachment to results is that it allows you to face your battles head-on, no matter the outcome. It makes you productive, proactive and free from fear. Fear of judgement, failure and all the rest of those obstacles that get in the way of you giving it your best shot.

This gives you the greatest chance of directing your strength and energy to what is important: the process. If you focus on the process with the strength of a 'big bang', who knows what that can produce? Perhaps a whole new universe.

Pade, Pade – Step by Step

We live in a world of instant gratification. If we can't have it now, we won't have it at all. Back in my day, if you wanted to see a movie, for example, you had to buy the newspaper, look up the time, call your friend on the landline, agree to a plan and commit to it. Then, say the movie was at 7pm, you would get to the cinema around 6pm so that you could queue up, wait your turn and buy a ticket with your cash, which you would have had to remember to withdraw from the bank. There were no mobiles, so you couldn't text your friend on the way and say: 'Yo, not feeling it. Raincheck?' or 'Late. Soz. K?' No, it wasn't 'K', because if you were late, there were probably no seats left, especially if it was a new release. So sad, too bad. You missed out.

But, these days, everything is a click away so everyone wants it now. Career, happiness, friendship, love. We don't want to have to work for it. Hell no. This way of life is incredibly problematic in so many ways, including messing with our sense of satisfaction. But where it really undoes us is in the uncomfortable moments on the battlefield, when we can't just close the tab or click the check-out button. We are so used to skipping all the juicy in-between moments – the glorious limbo transition stages – so we are not adept with the concept of step by step. And yet, it's all we can do.

Everything has steps and stages. Cooking is a great example. When I baked G's sliding Mentos cake, there were steps to take and an order to the process. You can't miss a step, or it just doesn't work. When we rush ahead and do things, instead of focusing on the next best step, it inevitably ends in tears. Or Mentos sliding off warm icing.

Back to *Frozen 2*. In the climax of the story, Elsa has left poor long-suffering Anna behind with her BFF, Olaf, who happens to be a snowman. As they find themselves in a deep, dark cave, Elsa's magic wears off, causing Olaf to melt, and Anna finds herself having lost everything. We've all had that moment, when the loss and grief floor you and you just don't know what to do. This is the moment on the battlefield when the warrior can't go on, but has to and therefore must choose what the most skilful action is from here. Thanks to Disney, the wisdom Anna gains in that moment is embodied in her song, which is so aptly called 'The Next Right Thing'. Because that's all we have to figure out in any given shitshow moment.

Let that serve to liberate you in those moments when you are lost, hopeless and don't know how the hell you are going to face the mammoth task in front of you. Use your tools – pull in, get clear and do the next right thing.

As my teacher Manorama used to say, '*pade, pade*'. Step by step. The next right thing.

Accepting the Self

One day, when G was four, we were listening to Bieber's classic (which he frequently requested) and, out of the blue, he asserted: 'Everyone really should go and love themselves, shouldn't they Mum?' Yeah, they should.

Loving yourself doesn't mean going to Kanye or Trump extremes. It doesn't mean putting on your costume and looking in the mirror, high-fiving yourself. It's not about ego, arrogance or selfishness.

Self-love has nothing to do with baths or day spas. Those things are nice, but they're not going to unravel the deep lack of self-worth and self-hatred within that we carry around and project onto the people around us.

Loving the self as it is, in the present moment, is radical self-acceptance. Learning to accept yourself fully – the good, the bad and the ugly – is no small thing. Working on being a better human while forgiving yourself for being imperfect is the key to your inner strength. Because we are all imperfect. Every single one of us. I know my strengths. I know my superpowers. I know I have lots of valuable and wonderful qualities. But I also know I have a massive shadow. You know, the not-very-attractive parts of yourself you try to wish or wash away with all the things? Of course, none of those methods work. They never will.

Shadow only exists because of light. All of your light, all of your goodness, has a flip side. It's the natural order of things – the sun and the moon, yin and yang, inhale and exhale. The only way out of self-hatred is falling in love with the self. All of the self. Wake up. Take conscious action. Do your best. Accept the rest.

Love yourself. Boundlessly. Like a Belieber loves Bieber.

This Moment is Your Guru

'Gurus' have received a lot of bad press over time. But a guru isn't just a spiritual teacher wearing robes. In Sanskrit, *gu* (like goo) can reference our darkness and *ru* can be understood as 'to remove'. So, a guru is anything that removes your darkness.

Isn't that liberating? That anything that shows your shadow, or sheds light on where you still have work to do, can be a teacher? Ultimately, the more you wake up and live in the present moment, the more each second of your life becomes a teacher.

Your family, the world in which you live, the people who surround you, the barista, your co-workers, the good stuff, the bad stuff, the illness, the feeling of connection, the sunsets, the rain, the rainbows ... *all* of it. As my teacher Manorama used to say: in every experience, ask yourself, 'What can I learn from this I could learn in no other way?' This is the best question to ask on the battlefield. Because, let's face it, life is gonna be turned upside down and inside out at some point for all of us. But can we use it to grow? Can it become our teacher? Can we allow it to remove our 'goo' instead of making us gooier?

The Laws of Manifestation

The manifest world is constantly moving through cycles of creation, sustenance and destruction. Things begin, they are sustained for a while and then they end. That's the deal. That's the process of living this thing called 'life'. A lot of our pain and frustration arises when we are fighting whatever part of the cycle we are in.

As I write this during the pandemic, I think it's fairly obvious which part of the cycle the world is in right now. If this shitshow isn't mass destruction on a global scale, I don't know what is. But through all of the devastation and contraction, there have been silver linings. It's wonderful that so many of us have discovered incredible gifts throughout the process. It's great if COVID has left you feeling creative and productive.

However, if during times of destruction you're reeling, if during lockdowns all you are capable of doing is the bare minimum, that's okay. That is natural. When things are falling apart, being dismantled or ending, it's normal to feel overwhelmed and sideswiped or like you're just not ready to get back up and keep on keeping on. It is not the time to welcome in the new dawn. Make no mistake, you will in due course. That day will come and, when it does, you will put on your dancing shoes and be oh-so ready. But in the process of destruction, lie on the floor. Literally get grounded. Rest as much as you need. Grieve, cry, surrender. Feel all the feels and make sure you get all the support you need. Denial and avoidance won't help you. Surrender and acceptance will.

It's only when you immerse yourself in the destruction and allow the ending that you will muster the strength to start again. In order to move into the creation phase, you must complete the last cycle. Allow yourself to be in the contraction of the ending phase. Don't fight it, allow it. If you try to force creation, new beginnings or productivity too early, that strength won't be fully accessible. And you need all your creative energy to build the new. Creative phases require so much of us. Then, we get a break in the sustenance phase, when things are just trucking along. (I'm always suspicious of that phase – when things are going well and there's no drama – because I know what's coming!) It's a good way to keep me enjoying every precious moment of those times that give us hope and bolster us.

Be in each part of the natural cycle of life. Accept that things begin, have a middle and inevitably end. You don't need to enjoy every stage. You just need to surrender to the ever-changing nature of being alive, slipping through our fingers like sand. Don't hold on to the sandcastles. Build them and let them wash away.

Key Takeaways

- Be a warrior of being in the atha, or present.
- Life doesn't want your perfection. It wants your presence. Just stay awake.
- Get out of the 'buts', off your butt and into acceptance of what is.
- Surrender doesn't mean giving up. Do the work, then let go and let God.
- Don't attach to results. Use that energy to stay in the process.
- *Pade, pade*. Step by step.
- Baby, you should really love yourself – the good, the bad and the ugly. Self-love is a form of radical self-acceptance.
- This very moment is your teacher.
- Things begin, have a middle and they end. That's the nature of life. Be completely in whichever part of the cycle you are in.
- Don't hold on to sandcastles. Build them and let them wash away.

REFLECTION QUESTIONS

1. Where in your life have you got stuck in the 'buts'? What would getting out of the 'buts' and into acceptance involve?

2. Think of something you are putting work into, such as a relationship or a project. What would you do differently if you had absolutely no attachment to the outcome? How would it free you?

3. Is there something you haven't done, but would do, if you had no attachment to results?

4. Which parts of yourself do you push away or loathe? Can you shed some light on those shadow parts of yourself and tell them how loved they are?

5. What's the big teacher in your life right now?

6. Which part of the cycle of manifestation do you struggle with the most? How can you bring more acceptance to it and embrace those moments? Think practically.

EXERCISE
OPEN-AWARENESS MEDITATION

In an open-awareness meditation, rather than focusing on something, you allow the mind to be free and expansive while becoming aware of all that arises. What arises could be sounds, feelings, thoughts or sensations. You become *choicelessly* aware of whatever arises in your consciousness. You follow whatever is most prominent. It might be a sound or a feeling.

Choose a comfortable seat and listen to the sounds around you. See if you can drop the separation of you and listening, and just totally be in hearing. Maybe you notice thoughts arise. Let them bubble up and let them move on. Expand your awareness to notice the air around you. Notice the breath. Notice physical sensations. Maybe the heat or cool on your skin. Notice thoughts and feelings as they come up. Feel it all, simultaneously. Rest in the awareness of holding it all. In a way, there is no method or technique. We simply stay aware.

It can be challenging to practise this style of meditation, as the mind may easily wander and be distracted when not anchored by a focus point. So, it's not the first stop for meditation as a general rule. Initially, the mind needs to be trained to concentrate through other forms of meditation, and then the technique can be introduced in stages. It's better to begin with a shorter time period and extend it as you become more able to expand your awareness and embrace everything that arises.

CHAPTER 13

The Six Cs to Find Your Strength

'The courageous heart is the one that is unafraid to open to the world, to care no matter what.'

Jack Kornfield

Clarity

'We don't see things as they are, we see them as we are.'

Anaïs Nin

Let's go back to the 'monkey mind', or the mind's tendency to move around. These movements create the way you see the world. Everything you experience in life moves through the lens of your unique perception. The problem with this is that you never really see clearly. It's like you're wearing glasses with fingerprints all over them. Your past experiences, false advertising (think social media) and imagination are particularly troublesome in colouring the lenses of your perception. They project all kinds of narrative onto whatever is in front of you and, therefore, interrupt your direct experience with it. The antidote to this, as always, is the atha! To stay in the present moment. To notice how quickly we make story and meaning out of everything and, instead, see things as they are by catching your monkey mind in the process of starting to swing from branch to branch.

Say, for example, you're on the dating battlefield. You're doing all the apps and your date game is strong. After wasting countless hours of your life swiping left, right and centre, leaving bad dates deflated, finally you meet someone. You like them and things are going well. Very quickly, you shift from getting to know who they are into a fantasy about how they could be 'the one', how great things will be, what you'll do together, the house you'll buy, maybe even the wedding and kids you'll have. Conversely, maybe things aren't going so well. They stop texting for a day or two. Very quickly, you're back on the battlefield. The imagination is set in motion and you're writing an epic (horror) story. Maybe it was from that comment I made. Maybe they lost their phone. Maybe they don't like me. Maybe they think I'm unlovable. Maybe they're going to abandon me. Maybe, maybe, maybe ...

When we're not in imagination, memory steps in. Most of us have been hurt by someone before. It's almost impossible not to bring in the scars of past relationship battles to the present experience. When we're getting to know someone intimately, we inevitably get triggered, the past informs the present and we armour up when there's not even a war on the horizon (although there will be, now that we've been triggered AF). Whoever you're dating can end up paying the price for all your past battles, disappointments and heartbreaks. It's not a great deal for them and it's not super helpful for you, unless you recognise your conditioning in the moment and use it instead to learn. Every date and every relationship offers the chance for you to see you where you are stuck, where you need to soften and where you still have work to do. Each moment is an opportunity to let go of the past and grow.

Whether you're dating, parenting, working or taking action in any other aspect of your life, it's up to you to notice when you are in imagination or memory, or misperceiving the world as we are prone to do, and pull yourself into the only thing we ever have, which is the now. Clean the lenses of your perception by staying awake and noticing how quickly the story tries to carry you off into an imaginary battle that doesn't exist. Instead, witness your life as it is. Not as you are. Put your weapons down, don't fight a phantom war. Save your energy for the real battles that lay ahead because, goodness knows, you'll need it.

Compassion

'In compassion lies the world's true strength.'
Gautama Buddha

One of the primary ethics of Buddhism, yoga, mindfulness and many other spiritual, philosophical and religious lineages is compassion or non-harm. Easy, right? Just don't kill anyone. I can do that. Unless, of course, I'm on an episode of *Game of Thrones*, in which case I'm taking my dragonglass and everyone is going down.

The problem is that, most of the time, everything we do creates a degree of harm to someone or something. It's almost impossible in the modern world to take an action that isn't affecting anyone or anything else. And sometimes, on the battlefield of life, you have to choose between a bunch of actions, all of which will cause a degree of harm. In these moments, the warrior needs to get very clear about which action is going to create the least harm. This is why it's so important to see clearly and consciously – so you can discern what the most skilful action is in every moment. How do you minimise harm? How do you stay compassionate while cultivating the courage to do what must be done?

We're not talking about 'idiot compassion', which Chogyam Trungpa Rinpoche so aptly coined. The tendency to 'do good' for self-gratification or to enable someone's behaviour. Warriors are not doormats. They have fierce boundaries and know how to say 'no' (they've slayed all the energy vampires, they have dragonglass and they're not afraid to use it).

Compassion from the perspective of a warrior is to get super strong and soft, all at once. It's designed to crack our hearts open, making us kinder and more courageous on the battlefield of life. It's used to endure life's inevitable heartbreaks without growing a steely prison around your heart where no one, and nothing, can enter again. (It's to *not* get all Daenerys and burn a city down with your dragons because your BFF was beheaded, your stalker died, you got 99 problems and Jon Snow is one). Compassion builds a bridge where there was once a moat. It's in our capacity to seek to understand things, no matter how challenging they are.

I have a dear friend, Fiona, who introduced me to her mantra many years ago. I use it frequently, but especially when I'm faced with challenging situations, when I really don't know what to do: 'What would love do?' It's so powerful, because when I ask that question in a tricky situation, I often want to rail against it. I'm like, *I know what love would do, but I want to throw it/them in the bin!* It's useful in bringing me back to my centre and seeing where I've created distance from someone or something, or where I'm closing off, so I can choose to stay receptive instead. And the process of asking the question always reinforces to me that love and compassion are generally the most courageous choices to make.

When you care deeply, when you are truly compassionate, it should not be viewed as a weakness. It's a superpower. Caring about others, especially when you see injustice, can be the impetus to take action and right the great wrongs. There's nothing passive about that. It's very active. In Buddhism, it's called the fierce sword of compassion and it has the power to change the world.

Courage

'Never succumb to the temptation of becoming bitter.
As you press for justice, be sure to move with dignity
and discipline, using only the instruments of love.'

Martin Luther King Jr

Compassion and courage are inextricably intertwined. It's courageous to keep your heart open once it's been broken. It's brave to stay soft in a world that's hard. And it takes guts to stay the course when the going gets tough.

When Gabriel was learning to swim, he used to be terrified of getting in the pool. As he protested in the car on the way to a lesson one day, I used the well-trodden explanation that bravery is being scared but doing the thing anyway. He wasn't convinced: 'That's stupid. Sometimes you're scared because you're going to hurt yourself.'

That's true, I thought, and so I dug deeper. Because it's not always a good idea to do something that scares you. Sometimes a fear is your intuition trying to keep you safe. I wanted him to trust his intuition. So, how could I teach the difference?

I said to G that he was right – he should always listen to his fear – but he could also stay open to the possibility that learning to swim, learning something new, was going to be hard. I could understand his fear. But by practising the discipline of getting in the pool again and again, in a way that made him feel safe, trusting his teacher and having a bit of faith, over time, I suggested, he might feel a little braver. This is where commitment supports courage.

Commitment

'Strength does not come from winning. When you go through hardships and decide not to surrender, that is strength.'
Mahatma Gandhi

Courage is often just about staying the course when we'd rather walk away. It's 'leaning in', as Sheryl Sandberg so famously framed it in her game-changing book that implored women to claim their rightful seat at the corporate table. Pema Chodron says we should lean in rather than backing out of experiences we don't like. Otherwise, we constantly find ourselves leaving the metaphoric room of our lives because it's too dark, too bright, too hot, too cold or too hard, instead of just being in the room, knowing it will inevitably change, as it always does.

It's staying in experiences – jobs, relationships, feelings – when they are uncomfortable, instead of escaping, running away or trying to change it. This is how we foster courage, resilience and strength.

Ultimately, courage will require your effort, discipline and, often, a leap of faith. It's about keeping an open mind and heart while caring deeply. If we can do this, we become the courageous warriors of the world.

Connectivity

'Call it a clan, call it a network, call it a tribe, call it a family. Whatever you call it, whoever you are, you need one.'

Jane Howard

There are times when the weight of single parenting feels heavier. The early years were tough, and lockdowns and homeschool have had their moments, but sickness is generally the worst. A few years ago, G had pneumonia. With a cumulative sleep debt I needed to literally pass out for a week solid to regain, and an inability to leave the house except for hospital visits, I felt very alone. I say 'felt' because that's the thing – feelings are just that. The reality is, I'm never alone. And there are always people to remind you of that. Often they are unexpected, and appear in the most random places. There were many surprise angels and moments of great joy during that difficult time. G lost his first tooth while in a coughing fit in the middle of the night, and we both laughed at me scrambling to find it among the sleep toys and phlegm. The staff at the hospital gave him a present for having such a wicked sense of humour, despite being so unwell. After being home for weeks, once he was feeling a little better, we dressed up as superheroes, did a dance to 'Ice Ice Baby' and posted it to Instagram at G's request. Vanilla Ice himself commented: 'I always wondered if Superman could dance, now I know and he picked the best song ever. LOL.' Silver linings in the strangest places.

And there's always something liberating about having to surrender, of not having a choice but to stop and let go of all the other things in life and practise selfless service completely.

It can be challenging and lonely doing it alone. In those relentless, exhausting, soul-destroying times of the tough, it is my community that holds me together. Those angels disguised as humans who appear in random places or text, check in, send gifts and insist on bringing soup and juice, even when I assure them 'I'm fine'. At the end of the day, the only reason I've survived the battlefield of single parenthood is because of my family and friends. The hours, days, weeks that my sister held G so I wouldn't break in those early years. The support my family showed me, in ways I never imagined possible. The SOS calls to friends when I just didn't have it in me anymore. My community is my strength. Without them, I'd be a proper shitshow.

That's what your tribe does. It takes care of the whole, steps up when you just can't, gives you strength when you don't have any and reminds you that you are never truly alone. Because you are part of the whole. Always.

Studies have illustrated that people who have satisfying relationships are happier, have fewer health problems and live longer. Conversely, those who feel lonely or isolated suffer from poor mental and physical health. We need to connect to others.

We can nurture connectivity in our lives in the tiny every day. Each experience provides the opportunity to connect or disconnect – with strangers on the street, in shops or in cafes. We can look another human in the eye, who is undoubtedly facing their own battlefield right now, and remind them they are not alone. Just with a glance, a smile or an acknowledgement of sharing this crazy thing called life together.

Even when we struggle with someone or something, we can always connect with a part of the experience. Stay open, curious and compassionate in your everyday interactions. In this way, we build bridges instead of creating more moats. Take care of each other, people. It's the only thing we really need to do in this lifetime, and we are generally not very good at it.

There is great strength in feeling connected to community – you can face any battlefield. But when you start to connect to the whole world around you and have faith, you become invincible. Because when you learn to dance with the universe, even Vanilla Ice has your back.

Curiosity

'I am neither especially clever nor especially gifted.
I am only very, very curious.'
Albert Einstein

Most of the greatest inventions throughout history are the result of an inquisitive mind.

Curiosity helps us learn, improve relationships with others, adapt to change and have a solutions-focused, problem-solving, growth mindset.

When in doubt, when all else fails, curiosity is the answer. When you're fighting a losing battle and can't see a way out, curiosity is your Batmobile. You can always seek to understand, instead of know. You can always listen, instead of waiting your turn to speak. You can always stay open, instead of closed. Curiosity is the ultimate superpower that keeps you awake and engaged.

Key Takeaways

- Clarity: Anaïs Nin famously said, 'We don't see things as they are, we see them as we are.' Start to clean the lenses of your perception so you can see clearly.

- Compassion: according to the Buddha, 'In compassion lies the world's true strength.' So always ask, 'What would love do?'

- Courage: courage is remaining soft in a world that's hard, and staying the course with discipline and faith.

- Commitment: commitment is leaning in, when you'd rather back away.

- Connectivity: community gives us strength when we have none. We can always choose to connect or disconnect from an experience.

- Curiosity: when in doubt, when all else fails, curiosity is the answer.

REFLECTION QUESTIONS

1. Where do you see the lenses of your perception particularly smudged? What gets in the way of you seeing clearly?

2. Think of someone you find it hard to have compassion for. See if you can seek to understand what it is that gets in the way. Stay curious.

3. Where do you find it hard to stay open and soft?

4. What are the situations or places you find it challenging to stay the course in?

5. Think of all the people in your community who support you in some way. What does community mean to you?

6. Think of something you find really hard to connect with. Is there some part of it you can seek to understand?

EXERCISE
BODY SCAN

This practice brings about a state of deep relaxation, providing significant physical and emotional benefits. You could record this as a voice memo, until you get in the habit of doing the scan yourself. You don't have to work in this order of body parts. It's more about inviting each part of the body to relax.

Lie down in a comfortable position on your back, with your palms facing up. Allow the feet to roll out gently. Feel the weight of the body on the floor. Notice the parts of your body connecting with the earth and relax, becoming heavier with each breath. Feel the bones relaxing down, flesh melting and softening. Notice the sounds around you, from the most distant sounds to those closer. Can you hear the soft sound of your breath, your heart beating, your blood flowing? Shift your attention to your right hand. And then slowly move your awareness to each body part, relaxing it and letting it go. Start with the right thumb; relax it. Then move to the index finger, middle finger, fourth finger, pinky finger. Then the back of the hand, palm of the hand. Right wrist, forearm, elbow, upper arm, shoulder. Right side of the waist, right hip. Right thigh, knee, shin, ankle, foot, back of the foot. Right big toe, second toe, third toe, fourth toe, fifth toe. Right heel, calf, back of the thigh, buttock. The whole right side of the body completely relaxes. Shift your awareness to your left hand. Left thumb, relax. Index finger, middle finger, fourth finger, fifth finger. Back of the hand, palm of the hand. Left wrist, forearm, elbow, upper arm, shoulder. Left side of the waist, left hip. Left thigh, knee, shin, ankle, foot, back of the foot. Left big toe, second toe, third toe, fourth toe, fifth toe. Left heel, calf, back of the thigh, buttock. The whole left side of the body completely relaxes. Bring awareness to the crown of head and scalp, relax. The forehead, eyebrows, nose, jaw, teeth, tongue, lips, chin, throat, chest, belly, pelvis. The lower back, middle back, upper back, neck. The front of the body. The back of the body. The whole body. The whole body completely relaxes.

Bring your awareness back into the space, back into the body, by focusing on your breath. Notice the sounds around you. Notice the quality of your breath. Take a slow, deep inhale and a slow, deep exhale.

CHAPTER 14

Authenticity

'If you make it a way of life always to tell the truth, then anything you undertake will have a successful result.'

Yoga Sutra 2:36 (translated by Geshe Michael Roach and Christie McNally)

Authenticity is defined by psychologists as the act of expressing one's true self. Research shows it has many psychological benefits, including increased wellbeing and positive social relationships.

In order to express one's true self, first you have to know what that is. Which is why it always comes back to understanding who and what you are. To live an authentic life, you have to connect to your own values first, then you can connect to others from a place of steadiness and confidence. You don't doubt yourself or get defensive, and you always stay open to understanding and learning.

Speaking Your Truth

Authenticity involves listening to and speaking your truth – saying what you mean and meaning what you say. It's a very powerful way to communicate because when you are connected to your morals, you can move mountains. The truth is a slippery thing because, as we know, we're looking at the world through smudged glasses in the form of our subjective perceptions.

It's been proven that no two people remember the same event in the same way. It's a phenomenon called the 'Mandela Effect'. Have you ever had an experience where you believed something was true with certainty, only to discover later that you were wrong? We must acknowledge that every person's version of the truth is going to be different, and it can change. My friend Noelle always says, 'When you think you *know*, look again.'

To truly say what you mean and mean what you say, immense vulnerability is required. Starting to peel back the layers of all that keeps us from speaking our truth takes self-study and courage. This is not what we've been taught or brought up to believe. This is not what we've heard from a friend or seen on Facebook. This is what we have spent time processing with curiosity, compassion and clarity. The world is no longer viewed through smudged glasses. We constantly clean them and, as a result, witness everything with a crystal-clear, present mind. From this place, we can speak honestly from the heart and soul.

When we become established in the practice of honesty, when we are honest with ourselves and others, we will succeed in all we do. Because as we are more genuine in our thoughts, communication and actions, those around us are more truthful and trust us in return. As we build trust in ourselves and start to live our truth, we become incredibly powerful. Watching someone connected to their truth and speak it, no matter how challenging it may be, is breathtaking to watch. They have the ability to change the world. Think of all the great change-makers who did this – Gandhi, Martin Luther King Jr, Mother Teresa, Florence Nightingale – each one had an unwavering sense of purpose and faith, spoke their truth and lived their lives by an unshakeable moral compass in service of others.

The world needs us to be everything we can possibly be. It needs you in your full expression and your full power. It needs you to be Elsa with her new frock. Then, it needs you to use your strength to serve others.

Selfless Service

When you use your energy to serve yourself, what the universe gives you will match that. It will be limited, providing what you need for yourself and you alone.

But if your intention is to use your strength to serve others, to serve all beings, then the universe will match you with that. It'll give you enough power to light up the world.

The most powerful thing about selfless service, though, is how it makes you feel. When you do something for the benefit of someone else, it's very hard to not receive a benefit yourself. Even if it's just feeling good about contributing positively to the world.

In the end, that is what it's all about. Just like the apple tree, the results of you harnessing your inner strength are not for you. After all, what's the point of being Batman; why have all those incredible superpowers if you're not going to use them to save the world?

Key Takeaways

- Authenticity is the expression of oneself. In order to express yourself, you must know who you are.
- Understand who and what you are.
- Connect to your values.
- Say what you mean and mean what you say; listen to others and really hear them.
- The world needs you to be Elsa in her new frock.
- Once you find your strength, use it to serve others.

REFLECTION QUESTIONS

1. Find a moment in the next week where you consciously go above and beyond purely for the service of someone else. How did it feel?

2. What did you find interesting about this process?

EXERCISE
UJJAYI BREATH

From a yoga physiology perspective, the *vishuddha* chakra (energy centre) is based in the throat space and neck, and is the seat of honest communication and expression. This exercise is centred around this chakra.

In addition, *ujjayi* means victorious. When we breathe in this way, we are victorious over the monkey mind and its tendency to whirl. We learn to surf on the waves and dive deep into the ocean of who we really are.

Sit with a tall spine and your hands resting where comfortable, palms up or down. Close the eyes and watch the breath. Place one of your palms just in front of your mouth, about 5 centimetres away. Take a slow, steady inhale through the nose and, on the exhale, breathe onto your hand like you're fogging up a mirror. Feel the warm air on your palm. On the next breath, move the hand slightly further away and repeat, seeing if you can still feel your breath on the palm. Place the hands back on your lap. Now, try the same breath but, this time, with the mouth closed. Add a silent, internal count of four on the inhale and exhale to the same count. Take a few rounds. Then, return to breathing as normal and notice how you feel.

Conclusion

'Thus, I have taught you the secret

Of secrets, the utmost knowledge;

Meditate deeply upon it,

Then act as you think best.'

Bhagavad Gita 18:63 (translation by Stephen Mitchell)

My journey with these potent teachings began decades ago, like Arjuna at the beginning of the *Gita*. I was 19, sitting in a psychiatrist's office because there were so many aspects of life that felt like a battlefield I wouldn't survive. I wanted to stop being at war with myself. I was tired of living in fear. All I felt was doubt, confusion and panic, just like Arjuna. The psychiatrist, Mark, asked me some questions and I did some tests. Then, he scribbled on a piece of paper, handed it to me and instructed me to buy what was on the list. I looked at my prescription: books. He gave me a list of books. Not drugs and not a referral to yet another doctor but a list of books on the philosophy of Buddhism and yoga. He told me there was nothing wrong with me. I just felt things in a big way and the books could give me some tools to manage those feelings. And so began my love affair with this ancient wisdom.

There have been so many times since that fateful day that I've wondered how different life would have been if I'd stumbled into someone else's room, if I'd thrown the list away, if I'd cancelled the appointment (which I almost did). Maybe the philosophy still would have found me. Maybe not.

I'm no Sanskrit scholar. I don't think I ever will be. I like all my Rachael-ness and the messy battlefield that is my life too much. I'm a proudly imperfect yogi. I have spent an inordinate amount of time studying and trying to embody these texts, on and off the mat, in an attempt to apply them to this crazy-ass modern world. (I mean, everyone spends their Saturday nights either drinking negronis and/or studying the *Upanishads*, right?) Because where else should they be applied other than in this mixed-up, shambolic, miraculous world we get to visit for a brief moment in time? What a gift to be alive. I don't want to blink and miss it. I want to live my life on Earth. I want to face the battlefields with as much grace as I can muster.

After all this time, I don't know how graceful I've become. In fact, I'd say that adulting has thrown me into a new realm of *Game-of-Thrones-*style melee, White Walkers and all. But what has changed is my capacity to access my inner strength and become a warrior on the battlefield of my own life, day by day, *pade, pade.*

Within a year of those early *Play School Live* touring days, my beloved grandpa passed away. I didn't realise it at the time, but those moments backstage with him, my hero and my teacher, were some of our final days together, and the most precious and sacred of my life. From the literal battlefields of World War II where he survived being shot down twice to supporting his granddaughter on her more modern battlefield of single parenthood, he was my true superhero. They don't make them like him anymore. I'm not sure they ever will.

I was fortunate enough to tell him all the things I wanted to in his final days. I told him I knew how proud of me he was. I promised him I'd stay strong. I expressed my gratitude at having him as an unwavering guiding light of unconditional love throughout my life. He was my Krishna. He was my guide. And, most importantly, I told him I loved him. He taught me that I had to fight but that, in the end, just like in the *Gita*, it all comes back to love.

There have been so many moments where I've wanted to give up. But every time I do, I picture my grandpa smiling and winking at me, and I hear him say, 'I will protect you, but you have to row away from the rocks, my darling.' All I feel is immense gratitude for that freezing Canberra winter that brought us together while things were falling apart. Because in that moment, I became the hero of my own anti-fairytale. I chose to find my strength and I said goodbye to the damsel in distress forever.

I'm still on stage, smiling and singing 'If You're Happy and You Know It.' It's a lie half the time. But the other half of the time – well, the battlefield is pretty damn great. And those days, weeks, months and years when it's not, I generally know how to access my inner strength. But when I forget, I have these teachings (and Disney films) that nothing, and no one, can take away from me.

In the end, as Krishna says in his final words to Arjuna, all we can really do is act as we think best. So whatever battlefield you find yourself on, that's all I wish for you: to find your inner strength, act as you think best and let go of the rest. You may lose your superpowers, you might get a new Disney frock or you could wind up having to find a goat's head, but you'll always find your way home, because you're already here.

GRATITUDE

How do we thank all the people who helped us find our strength in a few short paragraphs? I shall endeavour to put into words what really cannot be.

First, to all of my teachers. Anything in this book that resonates, or makes sense for readers, is thanks to you and these teachings. Anything that doesn't is due to the fact that I haven't fully integrated it yet. Given I don't have your dedication and eloquence, I'm sure I've clumsily fumbled through some concepts that will have you taking some deep breaths. In particular: Manorama D'Alvia, Maty Ezraty (how I miss you so much and hope I make you proud), Sharon Gannon, David Life, Jessica Stickler, Katie Manitsas, Katie Agnew, Yogeswari, Jules Febre, Noelle Connolly and Eileen Hall.

Special thanks to those of you who believed in me, and this book, early on, actively encouraging me to pitch it: Abbie Cornish, Toni Pearen, Jordanna Levin, Katie Manitsas, Isabelle Cornish, Lucy Lord, Emma Scott, my Aunt Dee, Jade Clark and especially Cassie Mendoza-Jones. Cassie, you'll never really know how integral you were in this process. Your generosity to so many fledgling writers is boundless.

To my family and friends: you are my strength. I love you like Elsa loves a good song and frock. There is no way I would have survived the battlefield of working single parenthood without each and every one of you.

Mum and Craig, thank you for your tireless support, having my back, and showing me the value of picking yourself up and getting on with it, after each defeat on the battlefield. I love you both. Always and all ways.

Tata and Nic (feat. Nanna Jodi), I wouldn't have made it through pregnancy and the first few years without your constant presence. Jadey for all the SOS calls and sleepovers in the Bat Cave. I am so grateful that you all loved G and me so fiercely in those early days and held me so I could find myself again.

Dad and Tracey, especially for those early *Play School Live* Melbourne tours (one particularly action-packed tour involved you putting on your gloves and washing reflux vomit out of a cast and crew rental car).

My yoga family: I'm so lucky to be part of such a supportive, loving, conscious community. Thank you for keeping me on my toes, showing me where I have work to do, and inspiring me to be a better person and student.

My creative sounding boards (especially Abbie, Tash, Danielle, Fraser, Em, George, Guy and Brendan), thank you for humouring me as I bounce ideas off you, and for championing my creativity in all the ways.

Noelle, Cathleen, Lu and Donna, my lockdown crew who were the cheerleaders of this book (and of G and me) every damn day and kept me laughing and writing when I wanted to cry and throw it in the bin.

David and Brendan, for being the first people to read the initial draft of the manuscript in the middle of a pandemic: two of the best people I know, and the most stupidly talented writers.

Nigel Watts, thank you for reminding me who I was when I'd forgotten.

My publisher, Kelly Doust, who believed in the potential of this book from our very first phone conversation. Kelly, thank you for encouraging me to see a bigger life for it than I ever could have imagined, and for guiding me every step of the way with your calm, confident warmth. To the incredible Affirm publishing family, you are a dream to work with, and all I have is immense gratitude for taking a punt on me and welcoming me with open arms, especially Martin, Kevin and Susie.

Ally McManus, the editor with the mostess, thank you for your work on the book and for introducing me to my Wellbeing family a few years ago. Terry Robson, Wellbeing editor, thanks for letting me explore my obsession and refine my skills in communicating these ancient teachings in an accessible way to a wider audience.

Most of all to G, who let me do an average-at-best job of parenting and homeschooling in lockdown while writing this book. We did it, buddy. We always do. Thank you for making me laugh every day with your never-ending supply of terrible jokes. May you find the strength to face any battlefield that comes your way. I love you the most.